The Stories and Recollections of Umberto Saba

The Stories and Recollections of Umberto Saba

Translated by Estelle Gilson

The Sheep Meadow Press
Riverdale-on-Hudson, New York

The material in this book was originally published in *Prose,* © 1964 by Arnoldo Mondadori Editore.

All inquiries and permission requests should be addressed to: The Sheep Meadow Press, P.O. Box 1345, Riverdale-on-Hudson, New York 10471.

Typeset in Times Roman by Keystrokes, Lenox, Massachusetts
Printed by Princeton University Press on acid-free paper. It meets the guidelines for permanence and durability of the Committee on Production Guidelines for Book Longevity of the Council on Library Resources.

Library of Congress Cataloging-in-Publication Data

Saba, Umberto, 1883–1957.
   [Selections. English. 1992]
   Stories and recollections of Umberto Saba / by Umberto Saba : translated by Estelle Gilson.
     p.   cm.
   ISBN 1-878818-21-X
   I. Title.
PQ4841.A18A23   1992
858'.91208—dc20   92-39319
                                           CIP

The Sheep Meadow Press gratefully acknowledges a grant from the New York State Council on the Arts which helped in the publication of this book.

Contents

FROM THREE FRAGMENTS

FROM SHORTCUTS AND VERY SHORT STORIES 1934–1948

Very Short Stories 1946

FROM ARTICLES

Introduction

A READER EXPOSED TO Umberto Saba's entire output, poetry, fiction, recollections, "shortcuts," and letters, would have a fairly clear idea of the salient factors in this deeply autobiographical writer's life: what he did, where he lived, whom he liked and disliked, what he valued, and what befell him and the Italian people during his lifetime. But though Saba is considered a major twentieth-century Italian literary figure, very little of his work has appeared in English—a short novel, *Ernesto*, was published in Great Britain in 1987, and a very slim volume of poetry—31 of the more than 600 poems Saba wrote—was published in the United States in 1980. In Italy, too, Saba's renown was a long time coming for reasons that have less to do with his genius than with the fact that he was born in a difficult time and place for an Italian writer and under circumstances that scarred his psyche.

Like his more famous countryman, Italo Svevo, whose real name was Ettore Schmitz, Saba was born a Jew in Trieste, and used a pen name. He was born Umberto Poli, the only child of the marriage between a non-Jew, Ugo Edoardo Poli, and Felicita Rachele Coen, niece of the famous Samuel David Luzzatto (see "A Hebrew Scholar"). By the time of his birth, however, on March 9, 1883, his father had deserted the family and (Saba writes) was thereafter referred to by his mother as "the murderer." In a letter describing the circumstances of his birth to a friend, written in 1955 when he was seventy-two, Saba still recalled his father's desertion with bitterness. "In 1882 there lived a man who sold furniture on the installment plan. He was a widower . . . the son of a genre painter (who I think did still lifes of fruit to hang in dining rooms) and of a woman (a countess) of the Arrivabene family. When the man was about forty years old, a marriage broker . . . proposed him as a match for my mother, who was not much younger than he. He was accepted. For four thousand fiorini, the wretch had himself circumcised, changed his name to Abraham (one can imagine with what hidden anger), and married my mother who owned a small furniture store at the time."

For a time Saba and his mother lived with an aunt, Regina Luzzatto, the beloved, hardworking Aunt Regina to whom *The Jews* is dedicated. Eventually Rachele Poli, who had to support herself and her child, left the boy in the care of a Slovenian Catholic nursemaid, Giuseppina Sabar, who had lost her own child and who became a second mother to "little

Berto." One of Saba's earliest memories was of his crying in the nurse-maid's arms while his mother berated her. Although the nursemaid was forbidden by the mother to take the child to church with her, she did so anyway and instead of saying a Hebrew prayer, the "Sh'ma Israel" at bedtime, the boy learned to say the "paternoster" in Slovenian. Later however, he attended a "talmud torah" (Jewish school). Saba's affection for the warm, cheerful Sabar conflicted with his feelings for his unhappy mother. But Rachele Poli's tragedy became the central trauma of young Umberto's life. In a poem entitled "Autobiografia" he describes the mother "who felt all the burdens of life" and the "lighthearted, vagabond father" who like "a ball" had slipped from her hands as "two races in ancient combat." Sadly, the field of combat was the soul of the lonely, sensitive boy. It was only when Saba began psychoanalysis with Edoardo Weiss, a disciple of Freud, and one of the profession's first practitioners in Italy, that he was able to obtain a sense of his own identity and to understand the origin of this internal war. Much of what he learned was "translated" into poetry, but he was never fully healed and until the end of his days was subject to emotional crises that sometimes necessitated his spending time in sanatoria.

The fact that Trieste's Jewish community, which numbered under five thousand people around 1900, produced two of Italy's most important writers, who neither practiced Judaism nor wrote under their own names, reflects the nature of the city itself. At the time of Saba's birth it was a place of multiple and confusing loyalties.

Trieste is situated at the northeastern extreme of Italy, with its face to the sea—the Gulf of Trieste—and its back to the Carso—rugged lime-stone hills. Across the Adriatic, a ferry ride away, is Venice, with which Trieste rivaled as a seaport over the centuries. By 1900, however, Trieste had won the battle. Though its inhabitants were primarily Italian and fiercely committed to joining the emerging Italian republic, Trieste was part of the Austro-Hungarian Empire. The Austrians, who had declared it a free port, settled themselves primarily into the shipping, insurance, and banking businesses in the city and introduced Triestinos to "Sacher tortes," waltzes, and cafés, as well as psychoanalysis and middle-European architecture. As Trieste grew and prospered, immigrants from Adriatic and Mediterranean lands disembarked daily along its waterfront to seek their fortune. When James Joyce arrived from Dublin in 1904 to teach

English (he lived briefly in the very building where Saba later had his bookstore), he was fascinated by the fezzed, sashed, and skirted Turks, Greeks, and Albanians who strolled the city's streets in native costume.

Even after reunification with Italy in 1918, locution and location kept Trieste a cultural backwater as far as the rest of Italy was concerned. Svevo became palatable to his fellow countrymen only when he was in his sixties and only after James Joyce popularized his work in France. Saba, whose early reputation in Italy rested on his poetry, was prevented from reading it on Italian radio because of his Triestine accent (at least so he says—he is also said to have had an unpleasant nasal voice). "To have been born in Trieste in 1883," Saba wrote, "was to have been born elsewhere in 1850." Nevertheless his work, which celebrates the exotic beauties of the city as he knew it in his youth, helped bind Trieste to Italy. In 1943, after Italy's defeat in the Second World War, Trieste was once more autonomous, though under German rule. It did not rejoin Italy finally until 1954, after threats (which terrified Saba) of annexation by Yugoslavia.

Hemmed in by a mother "who did not know how to live or let other people live," as he was by the sea and hills of Trieste, only in imagination could the youthful Saba escape. And though he dreamed of the "wondrous world" that lay beyond his horizons, whenever he walked alone from the village of Barcola toward the Miramare (the castle Archduke Maximillian had built by the sea), he was afraid he would not find his way home. In a poem called "Childhood" he wrote, "I identified with austere blackbirds. The bright boy I longed to be was a starling, but I wasn't. I sat talking quietly to a hen." (See also the story, "The Hen.")

Saba's adult life, almost devoid of external adventure, was equally troubled and restricted. "To talk about my father's life is almost an absurdity," Linuccia Saba, the author's late daughter and editor of his prose, told an interviewer. "The facts are few and well known. His life was anything but romantic."

Though Saba studied the violin and began writing poetry when he was about seventeen, his early ambitions were for a career in business. He attended the Dante A'Lighieri in Trieste, then, briefly, its Academy of Commerce and Nautical Science, and later worked for a commercial firm in the city. Subject to conscription in the Italian army, he served in the infantry in 1908, and wrote the sequence entitled "Military Poems." In 1909 he married Carolina (Lina) Wolfler (who was to become the most prominent feminine figure in his poetry) and almost immediately produced the long verse cycle "Trieste and a Woman," in which his feelings for his wife and city are intertwined. He was recalled to military duty in 1915 and, though he served behind the lines, suffered a "breakdown" which required hospitalization. When he returned to Trieste in 1919, Saba was still without a sure source of income and decided to use money left to him by his Aunt Regina to purchase the bookshop—"the dark cave"— where he was to spend the greater part of his life. (See "The Story of a Bookshop.") The store (bearing his name, still in existence at the same location) not only provided a livelihood for Saba, but became a refuge for him from the loudspeakers and street rallies of the early days of fascism. When the Italian racial laws were passed in 1938, Saba fled to Paris, where, cut off from language, friends, and family, he felt so isolated—perhaps an evocation of his childhood fears—that despite his lack of money and proper "papers," he risked re-entering Italy. The story of his return is told in part in "Portrait of Curzio Malaparte." Later, during the Second World War, Saba, his wife, and daughter lived in hiding in Florence, where poet and family friend Eugenio Montale visited them daily. Immediately after the war, Saba spent time in Rome and Milan. It was during this period that he met England's Duke of Norfolk. (See "Royalty.")

Saba's first volume of poetry, *Poesie,* appeared in 1911. He published regularly thereafter, almost a chronology of his life ("the poet of himself," Giuseppe Ungaretti called him), but found little acceptance from the Italian critical establishment. In 1921, the year his mother died—"I pleaded with her to take me with her"—he himself published *Il Canzoniere,* all his poetry to date. "Did you see how the critics treated my *Canzoniere?*" he wrote to a friend. "Every little poet in Italy has pissed on it." In 1924 he suffered another breakdown, "an illness . . . that doesn't kill . . . but leaves you a choice more painful and harrowing than any other suffering."

His reputation, however, was growing and he formed friendships with other of Italy's literary elite, including Svevo, Ungaretti, Giacomo Debenedetti, and Carlo Levi. In 1943 Cesare Pavese suggested to the publishing house of Einaudi that it issue a complete collection of Saba's poetry. This edition of *Il Canzoniere* appeared in 1945 and was regularly revised and expanded. In 1948 Saba, who still felt underappreciated, wrote the lengthy *Story and Chronicles of the Canzoniere* in which, speaking of himself in the third person, he explained the origins and meanings of his own poetry. Though informative, the work is far less graceful and convincing than his less "purposeful" prose. His collected *Stories and Tales* appeared in 1956.

Saba was sixty-three when he won his first national literary award, the Viareggio Prize. He received the Award of the Lincei Academy in 1951. And in 1953, after numerous postponements (he waited in Rome, worrying that his money would give out), the University of Rome bestowed an honorary degree in letters on him. He was a sick and sad old man by then. He absented himself from the last part of the ceremony in Trieste on October 19th of the same year, in celebration of his seventieth birthday, with the following words. "Old, ill and exhausted as I am (appearances mean nothing: there are equatorial trees which though they seem to be fully leafed are so ridden with termites—memories are my termites, seventy years of memories—that it takes only the slightest shake to fell them) speaking in public, and still worse, speaking about myself, is a torment."

During 1953, despite his observations about the torments of memory, Saba had begun writing *Ernesto,* a brief novel of an adolescent boy's amorous and homosexual experiences in the Trieste of 1900. He wrote with passion, "a dike has broken in me," and with enormous enthusiasm, "the best thing I've written." Yet he never completed the work and told a friend he regretted having written it.

Perhaps his judgment was impaired by then. He spent his last years in and out of sanatoria. Just before Lina's death, early in 1957, he retreated for the last time to the Convent of St. Giusto in Gorizia, about an hour's drive from Trieste. His most frequent visitor there was Nora Baldi (the Noretta of "Meatballs and Tomato Sauce," a widow twenty years his junior, who had become his and Lina's closest friend). Here, seeking peace among people who knew and respected him, and left him to his ways, he lived in a disordered room, its floor littered with cigars, matches, and ashes, its surfaces covered with books, papers, abandoned clothing, and wrote his last poems and stories. He survived Lina by only nine months.

Saba, who believed that poets were "irremediably infantile," met his father briefly when he was twenty years old and discovered that he had inherited more than his light blue eyes. "I saw that he was a child / and that the gift I have, came from him." But the longings to be free as a "vagabond," bright as a "starling" remained all his life only longings.

Instead, as Carlo Levi observes in his introduction to *The Jews,* Saba seems to have accumulated the cares and sorrows of the world. The Holocaust left Saba stupefied and inclined to silence. "After Maidaneck . . ." he wrote in a "shortcut." And it was only Levi's importuning ("God alone knows how much effort it cost me," the latter wrote) that persuaded Saba to publish *The Jews,* written with that delicate irony and humor he feared would be misinterpreted.

Like his poetry, Saba's prose, which Levi has described as rich, complex, and scrupulously realistic, is clear, true, and remarkably—for a man as irritable, reclusive, and easily hurt as Saba—loving and affectionate.

"Being loved," Nora Baldi said to him one day, "can create miracles. How can one ever deny that a person can be changed by an external force?"

"Stupid," was his response. "How can you be so stupid? It's true, love can create miracles—but in the person who feels it—not the object of it. How much unnecessary suffering we'd all be spared if only people understood that simple . . . truth?"

Umberto Saba was a man without pretense or pretension. Large canvases and tall monuments were not for him. Fleeting moments in small lives were. The honesty and directness that led Saba to write intentionally prosaic poetry led to highly poetic prose—these brief, deep stories, always about the human heart, almost always his own. No matter to what shape he wrought his small, clear pieces, whether ten-page story or two-line shortcut, he embedded in each a hard, gem-like truth. . . .

There were moments (as well as extended periods) during the past decade when I feared I was the only person in the world interested in seeing Saba's prose in English.

For the fact that this book is now in your hands, I would like to thank my editor and publisher, Stanley Moss for his unstinting efforts on Saba's behalf. I would also thank the creators and supporters of the Italo Calvino (Translation Center at Columbia University) and Renato Poggioli (PEN American Center) Translation Awards (both of which this work received while still in manuscript) for their commitment to literary translation. The mere fact that such awards exist provides impetus, encouragement, and opportunity for those of us—translators throughout the world—who drudge for love alone . . .

And most of all I want to thank my husband Saul.

—Estelle Gilson

NOTE:

Saba's unhappy childhood and his use of pseudonyms (Saba was not his first) have contributed to an error in both Italian and English critical apparatus about his choice of the name. Under the misapprehension that "saba" means "bread" in Hebrew, a critic more than twenty years ago put forth the suggestion that Saba's choice of the name relates to the substantive nature of his material and was at the same time a gesture of fealty to his mother. This notion has been repeated without examination in critical and biographical publications. In fact "saba" does not mean "bread" in Hebrew. In a letter Linuccia Saba explained that Saba chose the name "after many trials when he suddenly recalled the beloved person of his earliest years, his nursemaid, Sabar."

The Jews

1910–1912

On an Early Manuscript by Saba

ONE DAY LAST MONTH I received a package from Trieste, which from its extraordinarily meticulous wrappings—the precision of its paper folds, and the twistings of its twine—I immediately recognized as the work of the famous Carletto, once assistant, then co-owner of Umberto Saba's antiquarian bookshop, whose thirty years of preparing such packages bespeaks a soul so unalterably and scrupulously reliable that it verges on the poetic. On opening this craftsman's masterpiece, I found an enchanting surprise: the manuscript of an unpublished book by my friend Saba. He wrote that while rummaging among his old papers, he had come across these early pieces dating back to 1910, to which he had added others from the same period or just a little later. He asked me to read the manuscript and keep it. It was a gift, a token of his friendship. And immediately on my first reading, I saw that it was a glorious and touching gift. In this almost half–century old prose I found a complete and perfect prefiguring of both the poet and the man; his pale blue glance, a glance of kindness, if kindness is the loving understanding of things, together with a fond and sharp-eyed clarity, and that superb sense of humor which, as he himself wrote about Svevo, "is the highest form of kindness." And all this set in a rich and complex prose of such scrupulous realism that it recalls Goethe or Thomas Mann, but is so much more brilliant, modern, and nervous, and unencumbered by German self-complacency. Therefore it seemed imperative to me that these writings, hidden for so many years, no longer be kept secret. I managed to persuade Saba (God alone knows how much effort it cost me, and how many of his scruples I had to overcome) to publish a part of it, the section that appears here entitled *The Jews,* which, comprising stories and tales, and almost the fragment of a great novel, is the loving description of a distant world of memory, one that nevertheless belongs to us and lives in our hearts.

Saba is old and sick; and the world's sorrows, the sorrows of existence, seem to have gathered in him more than in others with an unbearable intensity, as if he were the porous soil of a great denuded mountain which, unprotected and open to the storms, becomes saturated with the waters of muddy streams and the interminable rains of autumn. And as the bare soil of the mountain filters the turbid waters with which it is soaked and returns them to sunlight as clear springs, so it is that Saba, whose life has absorbed so much sorrow, gives us back in his works (as all the great Italian poets have done) only clarity and limpid serenity. Thus, in this prose, even the dark, insecure, and self-contained world of the Jews of Trieste's old ghetto appears clear and serene. And the depiction seems to spring from, more than mere mastery of art, that poetic kindness which takes on the pain of others, along with a kind of gratitude.

This is a world perceived as archaic and original, truly a world of kings, of poorly clothed kings, whose pains and sorrows are assumed by the poet and held within him, to be purified and returned to us, wrapped in affectionate irony, woven with patience and hope, and for all the misery of poverty, with the anxious certainty of being God's chosen.

This 1910 prose gives us the subject matter fully developed in another form which was to become one of the voices of Saba's poetry so many years later.

> The oldest went shopping alone
> perhaps more for pleasure than thrift
> For two fiorini he would take a capon home
> in his large, deep blue handkerchief.
>
> How beautiful my city must have been then
> all of it, an open marketplace.

So many people in these stories seem to emerge from that deep blue handkerchief, but first we meet his Aunt Regina,

> . . . an aunt as benevolent and beloved
> as a mother,

with that wonderful phrase, "the money on the wardrobe,"[1] which for Saba later becomes, and which really is, the "timid, touching, feminine plea, the plea of an old woman who expected not to be heeded." Only

---

[1] Saba's first earnings as a fifteen-year-old boy. See "Dedication to My Aunt Regina." The incident is also treated fictionally in the story "The Hen."

love reveals the true meaning of things, sweetens even unpleasant memories, surroundings, people, and every character from the well-known scholar Samuel David Luzzatto, the celebrated Shadal, to that extraordinary figure of the nineties, Uncle Edoardo, who, despite his horrible behavior, is nevertheless described with the same love (and the same linguistic pleasure) as the soldiers Zaccaria and Nino,[2] as Nino of the "despr't life," as Zaccaria of the "hart that conkers many harts." In this world women are as cloistered and safe as modest angels; and from Sofia, to Annuccia, to young Matilda, despite their meager and impoverished existence, they create a true maternal world.

The conflicts, terrors, quarrels, the "ancient combat" of the two races,[3] have been absorbed into the background and do not appear in this prose, just as they do not appear in Saba's poetry. It is as though characters in the narrative, who are so true, clearly differentiated, and described down to the smallest of their eccentricities and peculiarities, are enclosed in an atmosphere that unites them and makes them seem even truer. It is the atmosphere itself, which speaks through the poet in "Three Roads" from *Trieste and a Woman.*

> The old cemetery
> of the Jews, so dear in my thoughts
> when I think of my ancestors, after so much
> suffering and selling, buried in that place
> so alike in soul and face.

What makes this honesty possible, what transforms these tales into true stories, is the feeling, implicit in all of Saba's work and made explicit in his most recent poems, that what the world seeks, what it needs, is

---

[2]The eponymous protagonists of poems from the collection *Poetry Written during the War,* in which Saba used the two soldiers' own speech to powerful dramatic effect.

[3]Saba described his non-Jewish, vagabond father as a "ball" that slipped away from his unhappy Jewish mother who "felt all the burdens of life." The "two races in ancient conflict" form the two poles of conflict within the poet.

friendship. Should old Saba want to look back at his life with his ancient eyes of a juvenile, and write about it, he would, I think, tell us, with deepest friendship born of deepest sorrow, the true story of our era.

Carlo Levi

Rome
March 18, 1953

Dedication to My Aunt Regina

DEAR AUNT REGINA,

Permit me to dedicate to you, to your sweet, frugal, hardworking soul, these few, and I hope innocent, tales and recollections, many of which—the very first—were written over forty years ago, when you were still living.

In spite of your passion for saving and thrift (fairly common—however—when coins were made of gold), you didn't hesitate to take in my mother and me when we were in need. You took us in, you loved me, you gave me every necessity. There were fewer luxuries (sweets, they said then, were bad for children), but you were the first to deprive yourself of them. Of the many wonderful memories I have of you, one has remained fixed in my mind. When my mother decided to interrupt my studies and to place me as an apprentice with a trading house, I received after a trial period of several months (six, I think) my first monthly pay—ten crowns. I was (relatively speaking) a good boy (that is, a boy who wanted to be loved); so the idea of giving you all of my first youthful earnings thrilled me. So much so, that on leaving the office for home that evening, I walked quickly, almost ran, to get home early and give you and my mother what I thought was a completely unexpected pleasure. But I had hardly set foot in the house, I hadn't said one word, when you (who already knew about it, I don't know how, perhaps a letter from my employer), turned toward me and in a peremptory tone, with an unusually severe look on your face, said, "The money on the wardrobe." It was precisely through your words that the devil tempted me. The world (packed full of adults, each of whom, or so I thought, knew his humble or high business to perfection; many were geniuses; but all, geniuses or not, should have recognized my existence, which, instead, they seemed to consider unimportant) was so beautiful, so "green," so full of wonders! And there were so many things, so many pleasures my money could buy. I didn't put the money on the wardrobe. I rushed out of the house as if pursued; and the next morning I awoke without a penny, full of remorse, sorrow, disgust (also a little fear). How much better it would have been if I had listened to you! Because—I understood it too late—what had seemed to me then an inconsiderate and unjust order was actually the reverse, a timid, touching, feminine plea, the plea of an old woman who expected not to be heeded. And that's why this, which might seem to be an unpleasant memory, is instead one of the sweetest that you left me, one that I recall with the most pleasure.

You loved me—as I said—a great deal (perhaps more than my mother),
and you were the only one in the family happy to listen to my first poems
and stories. But you used to warn me that with poetry, and poetry alone,
I would never make enough to live on. And I followed (partly intuitively,
partly by chance) your advice. After having lived for a long time—too
long a time—at your expense, I bought (immediately after the First World
War, with money that you had left me, which—alas!—was no longer
gold; nevertheless, still with your help) that antiquarian bookstore on the
Via San Nicolò, which was perhaps nothing more, during the many years
I owned it, than a continuation, with a different appearance and contents,
of your shop on the Via di Riborgo, where old things were also bought
and sold. "It's harder to buy than sell" was yours, then mine, now one
of Carletto's business maxims. Perhaps—*Canzonieri* apart—I've followed, more than I realized, in your footsteps.

Your affectionate and grateful nephew,

Umberto

Trieste
December 3, 1952

Saba's note: The story of these first ten crowns—of a boy's first earnings—appears
in another version I call "The Hen," whose protagonist's name is Odone. But Odone
is, in part at least, a fiction. In reality, things went as described above.

Preface

I USED TO RECALL THESE STORIES written more than forty years ago as an incubus. They were, along with others, or so I thought then, to form a thick volume; but I never finished any except the sketches (complete in themselves) collected here, which I recently found purely by chance while rummaging through old papers. Rereading them, I liked them, perhaps even more than when I worked on them.

I liked them but I still don't know whether I'd publish them. I won't be the one to decide the matter. Someone else, I hope, will do it for me. There's nothing wrong, when we get old, in letting others undertake the responsibility of making decisions for us, at least in practical matters. The five stories (if they can be called stories; in reality, they're recollections in narrative form) were written when anti-Semitism seemed a joke; when I was able, without remorse, to yield to a benign irony, tinged with hidden affection for people and things (literally, *the* people and *the* things) I knew and saw, or as was even more often the case, of whom I'd heard talk during my childhood.

My mother, as is known, was Jewish, as was her whole family. The stories have two sources: my reaction (tinged, as I said, with affection) for a way of life which wasn't mine, which in those days was already rare, and which used to astonish me as an added splash of color in the "wondrous world," and, I think, from a kind of nostalgia for my father, who wasn't Jewish, and whom I knew little and late. And also (perhaps most of all) from my nursemaid, in whose home I spent my earliest days and wrote, as I said elsewhere, "the first words on the first pages of the life of a man." The oldest childhood memory I have (and in it a complete drama is condensed) is that of a woman (my mother) standing in the doorway of a furniture store, threatening a blond child with her hand while the child cries in the arms of another woman (my nursemaid) dressed in bright colors, who is guilty of having taken me, despite my mother's prohibitions, to church with her. The unhappy outcome of my mother's marriage (she was abandoned by her husband a few months before my birth) had reinforced her religious and racial prejudices. On the other hand, I don't recall ever hearing her inveigh, unless it was about my father, against other beliefs and religions. Nor was she, as far back as I can remember clearly, overly attached to Judaism, whose practices, in the end, she barely if ever observed. The only thing she retained was a great admiration and veneration for the memory of her maternal uncle, whom the reader will find further on in the guise of "A Hebrew Scholar." His name was Samuel David Luzzatto, and he used to sign his works with the anagram Shadal. So deep was her veneration of him that one day when I said I would become "even greater than Shadal," the poor woman fainted as if she had heard too strong an oath. (I had just recited one of my poems for her, "Glauco" it was called; and as far as I was concerned, my hoped for "greatness" was to evolve in a different way from that augured by the rabbis.) But there's a reason, even for this; and so many years have now passed since what I am about to tell happened, that it seems permissible to speak about it.

When Samuel David Luzzatto was professor of Hebrew at the rabbinical college in Padua, my mother, then very young, lived for some time in his home. One of Shadal's sons was a medical student. From a letter and a withered bouquet of violets sealed in a very faded embroidered bag which I found among her things on the day (having reached approximately my present age) she died, and which I buried with her, I learned that the two cousins were not indifferent to each other. Along with the letter and the powdery flowers, I put a letter of mine into the coffin, in which I pleaded with her to take me with her quickly. She didn't listen to me. She didn't want to or couldn't; and I remained so many more years in this world that I witnessed (and also survived) its infamous horrors, after which all of us—victim and executioner—are, and will continue to be for many centuries to come, much less than we had been before.

One other thing: The poor people about whom I speak in these pages seem very different from others. They seem so, but they aren't. Much is in the setting, in the customs, in, for example, the red fez my uncle Edoardo wears in "Doing Good." And if he boasts of having saved a poor wretch without first asking if he was a "goy or iudi" (Christian or Jew) and of having even brought him a glass of water, I ask myself if the great Tommaseo, who wasn't Jewish, would have done the same for the still greater Giacomo Leopardi. Perhaps he would have done it; but in that case, he would, I'm sure, have boasted about it. And the Hebrew poetry "in praise of important people" that Shadal used to write when he was young is something many others have written, if not in Hebrew, in all the ages and all the other languages of the world. The same may be said of the shops in the old ghetto. Anyone who knows what retail selling and the battle between competitors is like (moreover, what they were like in the last century) knows that even here differences are more a matter of style than substance.

And that is all I can say about these few resurrected recollections and stories. I can only add, to avoid any misunderstandings about racial and religious prejudices—which are alien to my nature as much as is possible in human nature—that if I have always recognized the merits and faults of Jews (they are the same, at least here in Italy, as those of all other Italians and Mediterraneans), I never felt myself anything but an Italian among Italians. The rest, before human madness and desperation made a tragedy of it, was to me—I repeat with pleasure—nothing but a "splash of color."

A Hebrew Scholar

IT WAS 1823, an October morning in Trieste. A large carriage drawn by two horses was climbing the steep Opcina slope at a walker's pace. Alongside it on foot were three young men talking among themselves and with the occupant of the carriage, a gentleman completely surrounded by luggage. In those days carriages were to stagecoaches what express trains are to our locals, and the man in the carriage, Samuel Vita Lolli, a rabbi, was moving from his native Trieste to Gorizia, where he would spend the coming academic year teaching senior students at the Talmud Torah.

The oldest of the young men who were accompanying the rabbi to the customs barrier partly for the pleasure of the walk and partly as a mark of respect was himself already well known to Trieste's Jews (the entire world to him) for his erudition and his Hebrew poetry, written to celebrate holidays or in praise of important people. Short and unattractive, with a large head, he would, however, one day be known far beyond this local circle, for he was none other than Samuel David Luzzatto. Born at the turn of the century, he was then twenty-three years old and made his living teaching Hebrew and secular subjects to the children of the city's wealthiest families, to whom he was more often recommended for respectability and good character than for scholarship.

The other two walkers were still boys. One, a cousin of Luzzatto's named Mortara, worked for a stock trading house in Trieste, a city fast becoming an important commercial center. The other, Vita Zelmann, was a student. Zelmann had been entertaining himself during the climb, kicking as many pebbles as he could find down the rocky hillside strewn with violet-colored brushwood, and enjoying the sound of the miniature landslide they produced. Though it was an innocent enough amusement, it irked the man in the carriage. He needed quiet for the few moments that remained before he reached the customs house, as far as his little retinue had decided to go, in order to debate Luzzatto on an old topic with them—one in which they were both consummately interested, their irremediable disagreement on it having formed the basis of their long friendship.

It was Samuel David Luzzatto's contention that vowel points and accents had not existed in Hebrew writing at the time of the Talmudists, and the consequences he drew from this discovery argued against the antiquity of the Zohar, as well as the entire Kabbala. Samuel Vita Lolli, an intense, cheerless man who suffered from migraine headaches, irritability, and depression, was a fervent Kabbalist. He believed that man had the power, even the obligation, with the aid of his will and special rites, to raise himself to a state of pure spirituality and thus to enter into a rapport with the *sefirot,* celestial powers that derived from the Almighty. Luzzatto's discoveries disturbed him precisely because the conclusions conflicted with his own beliefs. He therefore opposed them vehemently, accusing Luzzatto straight out of being an enemy of Judaism.

"Where you end up depends on where you begin," Lolli repeated now for the hundredth time, "and if you deny me the authenticity of the Zohar today, there's no reason you can't deny the Talmud tomorrow and who knows, even the Pentateuch, someday. That would be just fine? Right?"

"Please do me a favor and listen," Luzzatto answered. "It seems to me you're looking at the question incorrectly. The primary issue is grammar. Why don't you show me instead, though I know very well you can't, in what way I'm wrong when I offer you proof, P-R-O-O-F, that in the time of the Talmudists, dots and accents were not yet used in the Bible, and that therefore the Zohar, which refers to it in many places, must be the work of a later time and can in no way have been written by the authors of the Mishna and the Talmud. I say therefore . . ."

Samuel David Luzzatto, as usual, was becoming impassioned on the subject, but his opponent, also as usual, having nothing with which to oppose him except emotional arguments, turned suddenly toward his longtime student, Zelmann, who instead of paying attention to the learned dispute was persisting—the scoundrel—in the stupid and dangerous game of kicking stones with the toe of his boot. Leaning as far out of the carriage as he could, Lolli put his hands together to form a loudspeaker and shouted at the top of his lungs, "Zelmann is, was, and always will be a *hamor, hamor, hamor,*" which in Hebrew means "an ass, an ass, an ass." The poor boy, who hadn't expected the outburst and in whose favor it must be said that while amusing himself with the pebbles he hadn't missed a word of the discussion, became red in the face, at which that pernicious discoverer of the theory of dots seemed to notice him for the first time and smiled.

At the customs barrier, the yellow-and-black-striped gate opened to let the carriage pass, and Samuel David Luzzatto, consulting a large metal watch, announced that he had to return to the city. He would have been happy to accompany his great friend and critic Lolli much further, but at exactly eleven he was due at a new pupil's and had to be there on time.

Then Lolli got down from the carriage, embraced each of the three young men, and as if to excuse himself to Zelmann for the earlier "hamor" or to show that he wasn't carrying a grudge for the youth's tomfoolery, he added a smart smack on the cheek. Back in the carriage, he turned to stop the horses, which had already started to move, to exhort Luzzatto one last time (though in a whisper so as not to stir up the *reschmud* of the Slovene customs guards, anti-Semites being everywhere, even—just look at the dangerous deviations of this era—among Jews themselves). "May dear Luzzatto be careful about new ideas, so that his great talents do not do more harm than good to the already beleaguered cause of Judaism."

Luzzatto, very moved, replied half in Hebrew, half in Italian, reassuring Lolli as to his intentions. Then he suggested several times that the rabbi return to Trieste for Passover so that they could resume the interrupted discussion at leisure and celebrate the Seder together.

The carriage finally left and the little group began their descent to the city without heeding Zelmann's suggestion that they take a pretty little shortcut known to him alone. The air was still, the road deserted, the sea below sparkled in the sunlight, and the hearts of the young walkers—three, like the angels who appeared to the Patriarchs—stimulated by the discussion, the farewell, and the unusual, long morning walk, were, like the countryside around them, aglow. Vita Zelmann (who in the future would become the teacher Vita) no longer remembered the "hamor" of his own first teacher and, instead of entertaining himself kicking pebbles, suddenly became pensive, almost sad. The young merchant was thinking of how much money he could already have accumulated, easily and without risk (it was an old dream) if only his father had advanced him his part of his inheritance. Samuel David Luzzatto, who was already called "the great Shadal" by his students, was weighing the acronym with which he was already considering signing the writings that would, he was certain, one day alter aspects of Judaism and, with the help of God, restore it to its original eminence in the religious world. At present, according to him, everything was in complete disarray. He found faith altered and corrupted by the Kabbalists, the sacred scriptures defiled in places by copyists and commentators, grammar treated unimaginatively and without a philosophical approach, and literary taste in poetry and prose depraved. Then, suddenly hearing Zelmann's name spoken again by Mortara, it occurred to him that he had heard the name before and that it had left a favorable impression. He asked the boy if he were the Vita Zelmann who had been so outstanding at the Merchant Marine Academy that he'd received an honorable mention at the end of the year, an accomplishment in those days for a Jew at a Gentile school that had created a small stir among the town's Jewish population. The boy, blushing redder at this praise than at the "hamor" of his old teacher, said yes, he was the prizewinner. But it seemed to Luzzatto that he hadn't said it with a sense of self-satisfaction or with that poorly hidden pride of the very young when they can boast of an official success or even of a modest scholarly success. He felt, therefore, that he had to encourage the boy.

"Zelmann, you did very well to have distinguished yourself. As a good Jew, I'm grateful to you for it. We have to show our enemies that we value it as much as they, if not more. It's a shame that no one thought to put a notice about it in the *Corriere Israelitico* or in any of our other papers. Or perhaps it appeared and I missed it?"

The boy, quite confused, answered no, he didn't think there had been a notice. And besides, he didn't think an honorable mention was interesting enough to appear in a newspaper.

"I didn't say interesting, I said useful, and that's much more important. How old are you, Zelmann?"

"Sixteen, nearly seventeen."

"I'll be twenty-four next August. So you have to listen to the advice of someone with seven more years of experience than you. Now tell me, the way you'd tell your father or your friend here, why you're not more pleased with an award that you earned and that does you honor?"

The boy shrugged his shoulders, hesitating to reply.

"Don't you like commercial courses? Or do you dislike the idea of becoming a merchant?"

This time the youth looked at Luzzatto as if he were looking at God or at least a major prophet. Who could have told him? And if no one told him, how could he have known?

"But it had to be that. What else would explain your complete indifference, almost aversion? Do you feel you have a calling for a different vocation, one that's not in trade?"

And here Samuel David Luzzatto, who loved to talk as teacher to pupil with Jewish youngsters and who took pride in relating the hardships and privations he suffered in order to furnish his mind with the little he knew, which by then was bringing him both a living and renown in the community, told of the struggles with his father, a turner, who wanted him to be a mechanic and not a "haham." He began the story of how, as a boy, he had spent a few months apprenticed to a goldsmith, but only a few months. Day and night an inner voice was calling him to the study of Torah. And when his father would give him a few kreutzers to buy lunch, there were times he preferred skipping it and used the money to buy a book he needed. "There were so many things for a good Jew to do and to learn."

"Good Jews have always been good businessmen," Mortara objected. "It's only because Jews were bankers that they obtained the few privileges they enjoyed in the Middle Ages. Besides, being in business always leaves enough time to study Torah."

"Not for you," Vita Zelmann answered quickly. "You even work on Saturdays. I'd die of hunger first."

"All the more reason," Luzzatto interrupted Zelmann, "for you to be pleased with your prize. It goes to show that a Jew can fulfill all the obligations he has to, without transgressing the Law. But you're right too, Mortara. I correspond with a number of Hebrew scholars, who are also good businessmen. So was our great Mendelssohn. Didn't he have warehouses which sustained him and his children, and he had a good many of them—seven or eight, if not more? But things are different today. Who says he might not have accomplished still more, if more were possible, if the ignorance of his fellow Jews up north hadn't kept him from taking advantage of his own studies?"

"And you think you're as great as Mendelssohn?" Mortara asked, perhaps without irony.

"I don't think anything," Luzzatto answered, somewhat piqued. "I only think that when someone feels he has a calling, he has to pursue it without veering to the right or the left."

"And I feel the same way," Vita Zelmann declared with the affirming passion of a tortured martyr reciting the Shema Israel.

"However," the teacher added meaningfully, "you have to look into yourself closely, pass a lot of difficult tests, before you can be sure the calling really exists. Many times it's nothing more than a talent—in some sense like that of a music lover—a talent that can, in fact ought to, find its expression in some profession or other."

Mortified, the student was silent. Then he asked the teacher what nonreligious books he'd been reading recently.

"I am reading, rather, rereading *Moral Obligations* by Father Francesco Soave."

"By a Jesuit!" the two youths exclaimed together, sounding as amazed as they would have been to see a Jew cheerfully violating dietary laws.

"I don't know whether Father Soave was a Jesuit. And what's the difference, anyway? Can't there be virtuous men among non-Jews?" retorted Samuel David Luzzatto, who prided himself on his tolerance.

"All right, among non-Jews," Zelmann answered for himself and his companion, "but a Jesuit!"

"I'll say it again. I don't know and don't care whether Father Soave was or was not a Jesuit. But I still prefer a Jesuit who could write *Moral Obligations* to a Jewish atheist and pantheist such as Spinoza," Samuel David Luzzatto concluded—concluded quite cheerfully, having the kind of deep, abiding hatred for Spinoza that people have for persons and things they don't understand.

"But to get back to us, Vita. Not now, because the afternoons are getting shorter and lamp oil is expensive, but this spring, as soon as the days start getting longer, if you like, you can come to study at my house any Saturday after dinner, without charge, of course. I'd be happy, with God's help, to do what little I can for you."

Walking and talking this way, the three young men came to the outskirts of Trieste, and the free port town with its bustle and crisscrossings of new and noisy streets lay open before them. They separated at the first square; Samuel David Luzzatto, to go off and teach his new student, and the two boys, who were on holiday, to saunter along discussing—not without a great deal of quarreling and shoving—what each had heard and said on that memorable outing—and also, to tell the truth—other things of a purely personal nature.

Saba's notes:

Talmud Torah : Jewish religious school.

Samuel David Luzzatto: famous scholar and Semiticist. He taught Hebrew at the rabbinical college in Padua founded by Emperor Joseph II. Reference is made in this sketch to what appears to have been his major discovery.

I know that he was my mother's uncle, that he had two wives; one of them (the first) threw herself out a window, probably as the result of a nervous illness, although a cousin of mine (who later met the same fate, though through different means) assured me that Luzzatto's wife had done it because the great man was afflicted with an extreme attachment to the virtue of household economy, which meant (this is still my cousin speaking) that the poor woman (who would have been a wonderful cook) was rarely able to put anything on the dinner table but a dish known in Trieste and all of the Veneto as *panada,* made with dried, leftover bread, oil, and laurel (bay) leaves. Samuel David Luzzatto gorged on it and praised it as healthy and full of nutrients (today, we'd say vitamins). It is very good in fact, once in a while, and certainly healthy, but . . .

Like Mendelssohn, Luzzatto had several children. One of them, Benjamin, was a famous physician (an internist called into consultation from far and wide, even to the bedsides of heads of state); I still remember the astonishing effect it had on me in childhood when I heard tell (more than once) that when he died, the minister of public education sent a telegram of condolence to the family. Another son, Filosseno, had a sadder fate. Destined, everyone said, to be "the image of his father" and a second "luminary of Judaism," he died instead very young and in a tragic way. In Paris, where he was living in order to continue his studies, he quickly caught a venereal disease. Lacking the courage to tell his father (or even a physician) about his crime or its punishment, the illness spread rapidly with consequences one can imagine for the poor boy.

I know further through my thirty-some-odd years as an antiquarian book dealer (though I wrote this sketch in 1910, this note is being written in 1952) that there was always a market for Luzzatto's works; listed in a catalog, they always brought more than one request. His edition of the Pentateuch, with the original text facing, is particularly rare and recherché. Scholars and devotees both say it is very well done.

Reschmud: anti-Semitism. The word comes from *rasha,* which means "evil."

Seder: Passover ceremony (dinner) interspersed with various rites commemorating the flight of the Jews from Egypt.

Shema Israel: Hear, O Israel. The basic prayer of Jews, in which they profess their belief in one God.

Kreutzer: an Austrian coin. It was worth a *soldo* or about two cents.

Haham: a learned man (particularly in the terms of Jewish Law). "A haham, a real haham," my good rabbi said of me, going from classroom to classroom to describe "the prodigy" when, in my second-grade religious history class, I raised my hand to ask the (truly Talmudic) question: whether the rain of the deluge had begun drop by drop or all of a sudden. For which, you ought to know, my patient reader, I too was perceived as destined to become—far beyond a bank employee—a future "luminary of Judaism." If I am not, alas, it was (as I said in my preface) that "goy"'s, my dissolute father's, fault. Even more likely (given my father's absence) it was my nursemaid's fault. She was a Slovenian peasant who kept a picture of the infant Jesus (with whom I easily identified) at the head of her bed, and who took me with her every evening to the Church of the Rosary, which still stands in the part of the old city that was needlessly (I should say brutally) destroyed. Before I went to sleep, she had me recite the paternoster in Slovenian, instead of the Shema in Hebrew.

If, at the cost of repeating myself, I recount these things about long past times, it isn't—I swear, dear reader—to tell you about myself, but merely to lament those dreadful confusions that were possible in Europe, when Europe still existed, and in Trieste, when—in spite of everything, today as yesterday, yesterday as today—my most Italian of cities was in the ascendency. Then Adolf Hitler had to come along and "put things in order."

Trieste's Ghetto in 1860

TOWARD 1860, the dirty, exotic ghetto of Trieste was still in full flower. Though its Jews, both native born and immigrant, had for half a century been equal to other citizens and exempt from special taxes and humiliating badges, many had not overcome their innate antipathy to mingling their daily lives with the feared (and therefore hated) "goyim." This aversion, which wasn't religious, and which baptism didn't vitiate, was rooted in millenia of persecution and segregation, and kept even those families wealthy enough to live in new houses on new streets within the enclave where their parents and grandparents had been, and still were, selling secondhand items from the picturesque and disorganized stores in which their power was rooted. Newly built houses, though sound investments for widows and those fearful of riskier ventures, were, it is true, the dream of many, but they were bought for resale, their new owners preferring to go on living in their beloved ghetto, so full of warmth and memories.

Tradition and a sort of mental inertia had transformed this attitude into a form of obsession, a weight more easily borne than set aside. It became easy for Jews contemplating the world beyond their own to imagine the existence of persecutions which had ceased decades earlier and which, in fact, had never existed in that great Austrian mercantile port, whose population had too much of a southern character for the northern affliction of anti-Semitism to take root. And so it was that hardly were the ghetto doors open when upper-class Jews, those free of prejudice and fear, were able—either because of the power of their accumulated wealth or because of their historical experiences as a people who perhaps are more idealistic in business and businesslike in idealism—to leap directly into the most lucrative and influential positions in the administration of banks and of insurance and shipping companies.

It was a time when Trieste's Jewish community was growing with the daily arrival of Jews who, attracted by the flourishing and prosperous trade, were visibly changing the old fishing town into an enormous and tumultuous marketplace. Many who disembarked at the San Carlo wharf wearing red fezzes and torn clothes, with nothing more to their name than perhaps a letter commending them to the rabbi or some old philanthropist, turned up after a few years, sometimes after just a few months, in formal attire, including top hat, at services at one of the three synagogues, the Italian, German, or Spanish, two of which served the devout within the ghetto itself, while the third was close by in the Via del Monte.

The lower classes, people not venturesome enough to cut loose from petty dealings, went on doing business in the shanties of the piazzetta of the Jewish synagogue, or on the ground floor of the dank houses and brothels in the old city. Some of these stores, the size of cells, which produced colossal incomes, became legendary to the younger generation. Here, more than anyplace else, barterers, buyers and sellers of used clothing and furniture, battled out their disagreements in a business that has all but disappeared today. Customers were for the most part Slavs from the surrounding countryside or sailors from Illyria and Dalmatia, conscripts who needed a suitcase into which to put their few wretched belongings, or seamen who wanted to trade seedy clothing and worn-out shoes for clothes a trifle less seedy and shoes not quite so down at the heels. Larceny, swindles, and usury neither more frequent here nor more serious than anywhere else but more flagrant, more—to use a typically inappropriate term—"out in the open"—were practiced by all dealers, and to a greater extent by females, with absolutely sublime skill and uncanny insight into their victims' physical and psychological makeup. Every technique, whether for getting customers into their shops or for defeating competing dealers, was effective. The streets were narrow, the passageways crowded, and the open stores faced each other like enemy knights in the days when battles were won or lost in hand-to-hand combat. Passersby suspected of being potential purchasers were assaulted with the most brazen flattery, the kind streetwalkers used at night. If a young man came by, the female storekeeper would lure him with words praising his manliness, words that slipped easily from an indifferent enthusiasm; and she let him know that she herself was going to help him don the new pair of indestructible trousers which, because of her weakness for such a handsome blond, she was letting him have for almost nothing. But that "almost" was sometimes the total daily earnings of a family with eight children to feed, so that no one, once ensnared, ever escaped the trap, whether an hour or a minute later, without leaving behind some money. If instead of a young man a family man turned up, the brat scampering behind him was petted and proclaimed the best-looking child in town, with everyone wishing out loud to have one just like it; language, dialect, smiles changed according to the age, sex, and nationality of the customer. For more serious cases, when after long discussions a deal threatened to founder, hidden behind the counter was a last resort—a bottle of brandy and one or two dirty glasses. The dealers, husband and wife or mother and daughter, talked to each other during negotiations in a mawkish Triestine jargon interspersed with Jewish words, totally incomprehensible to outsiders. Still more frenzied was the competition between dealers, who often battled each other to the point of physical violence; and it wasn't at all unusual for the victor in a struggle with two or more competitors to be the one with the least flabby arm muscles and thus the greatest ability to drag the flattered, distracted, and unaccustomed-to-being-fought-over "goy" into his store. At this, an unsuccessful contender standing in the doorway of his shop would vent his fury, howling out his rival's business secrets and domestic depravities. Or, suddenly switching to complaints, he'd catalogue his own miseries and the number of mouths he had to feed with a primitive logic and flashes of eloquence worthy of Jeremiah. It was, in short, a battle for survival, as furious and fascinating as those one watches between insects of the field or shore.

But the owners of already established shops, those with steady customers, took pleasure in fulfilling their religious obligation to keep them shut on Saturdays, the Lord's day, when until sunset Jews are prohibited from any and all work, even tearing off a leaf or lighting a match. I myself have heard old people tell with pride and emotion how the crowds thronged the doorways of these stores Saturday nights, waiting for hours for the owner or his wife to open up, because, the speakers would add, those stores were blessed by God. They were a real promised land.

Sofia and Leone Vita

IN ONE OF THOSE STORES blessed by God and closed on the Sabbath, a young bride had been bustling about for several years. She wasn't really young, but that's how she might have seemed compared with her husband, thirty years her senior, if her wizened features and careless dress hadn't made her appear somewhat sexless and of an indeterminate age. With protruding eyes, thin hair parted horizontally across the top of her forehead from which bangs fell to her eyebrows, and a prematurely curving back, she resembled the waxen figures you see in exhibitions. And when she walked arm in arm with her seventy-year-old husband, proceeding slowly so as not to tire him, and pausing every so often till he caught his breath, that thirty-year difference in their age wasn't too striking to passersby.

He, crippled from birth, was even smaller and more shrunken than she and so nearsighted that he seemed to be peering through a slit. He wore in the style of the times a top hat and a long frock coat. His coat, however, was particularly soiled and so ill-fitting that it seemed to have been made for someone else. But there were plenty of dandies who, if offered a choice of winning the lottery or exchanging coats with him, would have opted for the latter. In the inside pocket of that coat, just over his heart, he carried a billfold, so stuffed with banknotes that from the outside it made a very tempting bulge. Leone Vita or, as everybody called him, Leone the Crutch, knew how to run his business. There wasn't a debtor wily enough to escape him, nor an auction from which he didn't come off with the choicest items. Just as a person who fears being attacked goes about armed, so Leone the Crutch, never sure he wouldn't run into a potential seller in the streets or at the Caffé Tergeste who might drop his asking price even below the minimum once he was shown the pistol of instant cash, always had his money at hand. But if he was a good businessman, he was also kindhearted. More than once that insatiable billfold was opened to help widows and orphans. He could spend a half day arguing over a minimal difference in the price of a piece of used furniture, but he could also, seeing the poverty in which a household would remain after his deal was concluded, leave behind a silver coin (Italian or Austrian) on that special table, which, properly polished up, would be featured in his store several days later. And wasn't he once assaulted for just such an act of charity by a young lout with too much arrogance and too little money, who slapped him in the face? Leone Vita wasn't at all ashamed to tell that story about his honest life and good deeds. As a matter of fact, he would cite the slap as irrefutable evidence of the ingratitude of accursed humanity.

He didn't do business with other Jews. Every poor Jew who passed him in the street raised his hat to him to the highest and every Jewish charitable organization counted him among its benefactors. When in synagogue he was called to the pulpit to hold the Scroll of the Law and was asked, according to procedure, if he intended to make a charitable offering in return for the honor, the figure he announced was always so generous that a murmur of approval would run through the congregation; and as he passed in the aisle, congregants would wave the fringed hems of their prayer shawls at him as a sign of blessing. It used to be said that Leone the Crutch was one of those originals; that after God made him, He broke the mold just as He had after Paganini or, to keep it in the family, after Samuel David Luzzatto, who was known as Shadal.

Sofia Angeli, who was related on her mother's side to the famous Shadal, was his second wife, his first having died some years earlier without leaving him any heirs. Because, in spite of his seventy years, he still enjoyed women, looking at them or being close to them, and because he needed someone to care for him nights and someone trustworthy to leave in the store during the day when he had to take care of other business, go to a religious service, or just play his daily game of dominoes at the Caffé Tergeste (his only vice—but no one is born perfect), he one day slipped a coin into an old rabbi's hand (without meeting too much resistance) and raised the subject with him. The latter first tried to kiss the hand that had favored him, then promised with the most solemn oaths that from that moment on he would busy himself with the matter with such zeal and discretion that he would settle the business quickly.

"Quickly, above all," Leone answered smiling. "As you can see, I don't have much time to waste."

"What are you talking about? You don't look more than fifty."

"But I'm seventy," the old man replied, extending his hand to his flatterer, who hurried to press it between his own and hold it there as long as possible.

"And what difference does age make? A man like you, Signor Leone, can find as many women as he wants who would be honored and happy to marry him. As a matter of fact, I don't think I'll have to look very far; perhaps I've already got our answer."

"Really? Who?"

"No, no, I can't give out any names yet. But be at the café tomorrow at this time, and God willing, I hope to bring you welcome news."

"Thank you, Rabbi. And if, perhaps, she's a widow, who knows? Maybe that would be better."

"A widow? What are you talking about?" the rabbi went on, sincerely moved and still holding tightly to that cold and generous hand. "We want a girl, someone pretty, from a good family and with her head on right, like dear Rachel was when you married her. King David asked for a virgin and he was much older than you, my dear Signor Leone."

The good rabbi, who realized that arranging this marriage gave him an opportunity not only to earn a large sum for himself but also to do a good deed, a veritable *mitzvah,* hadn't erred in his calculations when, that very evening, he knocked on the door where Sofia lived with her blind mother and a sister ten years younger than she. And he didn't have to waste words praising the groom. It was enough to speak the name Leone Vita for the three women to stand up at the same moment and to declare, each in a different way, her complete approval. The new bride smiled, turned her head away, and thinking not only of herself but also of the good such a marriage was certain to bring to her family whispered, "May it be for the best." Her sister embraced her with tears in her eyes, and her blind old mother called her close to place a hand on her head and offer a blessing. And the rabbi, who remembered having had her as a pupil in his Talmud Torah, added his blessing to that of the mother, promising that as a wedding present he would, with his own hands, write a *mezuzah* on parchment, which, sheathed in its metal case, was fixed to the doorway of every Jewish home so that, entering and leaving, its residents might have before their eyes and within reach of their lips a remembrance of the covenant between the Lord and the chosen people. The mother, after excusing herself for having nothing to offer him because of the extreme poverty in which the three lived, told the rabbi that if she could only marry off her other daughter, and embrace her son who was a soldier one last time, she would ask nothing more and die happy. But Stella, the younger daughter, who in contrast to Sofia was a marvel of a young woman and who had blossomed in that squalid place, after twenty centuries of persecution and exile, into a likeness of the illustrations of Rebecca at the well of Paddam-Taaran, contradicted her immediately. She swore, "on your life, mother," that she was happy to remain the way she was and that in no case could she be persuaded to abandon her mother, all the more now that her older sister would leave to live with her husband. Then the poor widow, overcome with despair, cursed herself and her life as nothing but a burden to her family. She pleaded for death with the most heartrending words and the most fervent prayers. The three surrounded her, trying to console and calm her, but managed only to press against her when she, in an outburst of gratitude and affection that would remain in her heart for days, kissed her daughters and the old rabbi again and again. The latter promised solemnly before leaving that when he returned the following day, he would bring the groom, who he assured them would not, as the blind old woman feared, be offended by the poverty of their surroundings. He would, in fact, considering his reputation for philanthropy, look upon it as an honor to help such a distinguished family and such an exemplary mother, whose son-in-law he would become as soon as possible.

Everything, in fact, turned out for the best, as Sofia had wished. This quiet woman of limited intelligence, who was perhaps incapable of passion, felt no aversion to Leone the Crutch, but married him and clung to him with all the affection of which her sweet, industrious soul was capable. And the kind old man, who could hardly believe his many blessings or that he had found such sincere affection at his age, immediately settled a monthly stipend on his mother-in-law; and in a letter in which she told her soldier son about his sister's marriage, he added, in his own handwriting, a note offering, as soon as the youth was discharged, to open a business for him of whatever sort he might want. Yet when, not knowing how to further demonstrate his gratitude toward his wife, to whom he had already given the most precious items he had culled from auctions and in whose favor he had redrawn his will, he proposed to move from the two-room apartment they occupied in the piazzetta of the Hebrew synagogue and to rent a larger and more convenient one, Sofia promptly rejected the offer, almost with indignation.

"Leone, dear, why don't we stay here, where we've always been so comfortable and rent out our small room instead? What do we need a second room for, when we spend the whole day in the store?"

Leone couldn't believe what he'd heard; it seemed impossible to have found such a treasure for a wife. He decided, right then and there, that the next day he would find the rabbi and, just like that, give him another fee almost as large as the first.

"But I was thinking of you, my dearest," he explained to Sofia, "so that you might have a larger house with a dining room and a maid's room."

"I have you and the business, that's enough for me," she interrupted him. "Why take in a servant, a goya, maybe even a spy? Even the day worker is too much."

And Leone hugged her to his chest, kissed and rekissed the hair on her forehead, exclaiming that if God had given him so much bitterness during his life, He must still really love him to have given him so much solace in his old age. It was praise which Sofia, proud and happy to have earned, used to repeat to herself. And to enhance the repayment of her husband's kindness, as well as to add to their wealth, she stayed in the small, damp, unhealthy shop from seven in the morning till nine at night without an hour of respite and with never a complaint or desire for anything other than good earnings every day.

But after the work week came the Sabbath, the solemn day Sofia and Leone Vita celebrated by going to temple mornings, then having lunch at her blind mother's, whom, despite her protests, they regaled with meats and confections. In the afternoon, they would either take a short, slow walk or, more often, fling themselves down on the bed to take a nap until sunset. That was the hour when the Sabbath was over; and after having been re-created in the image of the Lord, who had worked six days to make the world and had rested on the seventh, they would hurry out to reopen their store.

Giuseppe

TWO YEARS OF IDYLLIC HAPPINESS WENT BY, the only two such years for the Vita and Angeli families, who, though they lived apart, were in essence one family. Old Leone still had that bit of physical energy necessary to run a business. In fact, what with his enterprise and his wife's fervent sense of duty, his affairs had prospered to the extent that on August 22, 1862, by the Christian calendar or the twenty-sixth of Ab by the Jewish, Sofia Vita became the sole owner, free and clear, of a four-story house in the Via Pondares.

It was a building Leone had had his eyes on even before his marriage, and having seized an opportunity to get it at a good price, he immediately signed it over to his wife. Sofia was radiant that day, but hid her almost overwhelming joy or revealed it only in the doubling of tenderness toward her generous husband. He told her for the hundredth time how much pleasure it gave him to give a sensible wife who had brought happiness into his life something which, though an advantageous purchase, would have been depressing had he, an old man without heirs, acquired it solely for himself. And it was on this occasion that Leone Vita wrote his only poem, a Hebrew poem in praise of his wife, based on a comparison in a psalm—one between a devout man shunning wicked companions and a shrub growing next to a spring (by the spring he meant Sofia) which, without having to be watered, bore abundant fruit even in time of famine. The day the old man read the poem in his mother-in-law's house was without doubt the most memorable of his life. No poet ever enjoyed his success more; although to tell the truth, the three women, who knew only enough Hebrew to get through their prayers automatically, didn't understand very much. They were careful, however, not to let their ignorance show, and out of respect for the writer-reciter praised him to the skies. They even exchanged smiles among themselves from time to time, as if to show that they had appreciated the hidden and allegorical meanings of the composition. Although all three assured Leone that there was no need to do so, he had set his heart on translating the poem into Italian as well, which made the poor old widow cry and brought tears to his wife's and sister-in-law's eyes. But they were consoling tears, shed for happiness by these sweet creatures of the Lord.

The tears that were compelled by young Giuseppe's return from the army were a completely different matter. He had turned into quite a handsome young man, but how much worse his character had become! He seemed to have regressed to the years of his youth when he had behaved like the most dissolute and arrogant of all his companions, and his father, a dyer, had to drag him forcibly to Talmud Torah. The boy, who didn't want to go, would cling to every pillar along the way, planting his heels like a calf being led to slaughter. If his family relied on his fear of punishment and let him go alone, he would inevitably take a road that led to fields or wharves. On his return his father, who could smell out the scent of his guilt, would grab him, take down his trousers, and tie him to a winch in the dye works. Then he would beat him with a leather whip bought specifically for the purpose. It's true a moan or plea for forgiveness would have been enough to stop the useless torture. And though the scoundrel knew the recourse to be infallible, he was too proud to humiliate himself and never uttered a sound until he was close to fainting. But when his father died—of a stomach cancer, as the doctors said, or of a "goy" who opened a dye shop directly across from his, as his family said—and the boy had to look at him for the last time (before he was wrapped in his prayer shawl, within which, forever hidden from anyone's eyes, he would be lowered into his grave), his father's dried-up body and his yellow face set somehow in an expression of solemn sweetness recalled to the orphan an engraving of old father Abraham, and he felt irresistibly impelled to change his life.

And change it he did. For a whole year he applied himself so assiduously to his studies that his grades surpassed all his classmates', astonishing his teachers and the three community leaders who were in charge of the examinations. Then he immediately wanted to learn a trade. However, he didn't choose his father's; he wanted to become a watchmaker, although a seagoing career appealed to him much more. Nevertheless, he wasn't willing to leave his mother and sisters alone. He wanted to earn a weekly wage immediately—granted it would be small—to match the amount his family was receiving as charity from the community and Sofia's meager earnings teaching French and Hebrew to the children of a well-to-do family. Until he was twenty, he was a model son and brother, irreproachable except for his quarrel with a Gentile, who it seemed to him was following his sister Stella too often and too closely. Stella wept much and became very angry when she found out that her brother had stopped her suitor and had threatened him. Everyone else disapproved of his behavior, too, and considered the point of honor and his fraternal jealousy overdone. But it was a cloud that passed quickly.

The thunderbolt struck when the boy suddenly announced that he wanted to join the army. Although born in Trieste, he was an Italian citizen and, as the only son of a widow, was not subject to conscription. But he renounced this privilege. His mother's despair, his sister Sofia's pleas (Stella stopped speaking to him after their squabble), and the intercession of community leaders were useless. His determination was fixed, and he left just as he was becoming a veritable godsend to his family. On his return from military service and from Leghorn, he was another person. Or, more correctly, he was his old self, the one his father used to tie to the winch of the dye works and beat for his misdeeds. Instead of being grateful to old Leone for what he had done for his family during the years of his absence, he seemed to take a wicked pleasure in ignoring him or barely acknowledging him. And, in one of his first speeches to him, he made the shocking comparison between himself, Giuseppe Luzzatto, nephew of the great Shadal and warrant officer of the Royal Army (in reality he had been discharged a corporal major), and the gallant Medici captain, Giovanni dalle Bande Nere—Giovanni of the Black Bands—a comparison that seemed for a moment to bend the old man's shoulders even more, though it's highly unlikely that he knew of Giovanni's problems with the fainthearted Duke of Urbino. The women of the house appeared terrified of Giuseppe too. Only his mother dared to protect him. "Sowing wild oats," she said of his behavior, adding he would get over it once he had found a job and a wife. But the young man wasn't thinking of either. He hadn't even made up his mind to go back to work. He had forgotten his old watchmaker's trade, and Leone Vita seemed no longer to recall his promise to underwrite opening a shop for him. One day when Sofia tried to recall the pledge to him, the old man tightened his lips and said "no" with such firmness that she thought she hadn't made herself clear or hadn't heard correctly, and she repeated her question. But Leone didn't seem the least bit intimidated. On the contrary, he was so unusually resolute on this issue that Sofia became frightened and felt she would die on the spot.

"No and no again," said Leone. "Who cares if he's Giovanni of the Red Bands, I am Leone Vita. Oh, Lord."

"Don't get upset, my dear, my darling. No one wants to make you do anything you don't want to do. Even though you made verbal and written promises, I'm telling you, they're gone. You're the only master."

"I do believe so." And that "I do believe so" was said in such a way that it sickened Sofia, and right then and there she offered to give him back the house in the Via Pondares. "Are you trying to kill me?" she asked, going into the other room to get the deed. But when she returned with it, the old man was no longer there; and Sofia reproached herself for having lost her self-control, as if for an unforgivable crime. They reconciled that evening. And Leone promised her that if her brother were to show proof of reform and commitment to any kind of work at all, he, Leone Vita, would reinstate his promise. He added that though he wasn't Giovanni of the Red Bands, he was a man who didn't go back on his word. But he would appreciate it if they didn't speak about Giuseppe anymore until he had given the required proof. Further, he asked his wife to discourage her brother from spending so much time in his store, especially when he, Leone, was not there. The store was small enough already without having to accommodate extra loafers. Sofia didn't answer, but yawned to cover a smile and assured her husband that things would be done the way he wanted them to be. In reality, she had a plan.

Sofia knew what she was smiling about. Her brother wasn't spending all that time in their store because he was so fond of his brother-in-law or even of her. He had another interest, the proprietress of the store across the street, who was also married to an old man—the latter full of pimples and wrinkles—and who, when she wasn't taking care of customers, would sit in the doorway of her used clothing shop. She was very short but quite attractive, and as quarrelsome as one of those hummingbirds which in mating season are fiercest to one another. Giuseppe would walk back and forth between his brother-in-law's and the little shopkeeper's store, and pretending that he was keeping his sister company, he spent hours sitting across from the woman. This had been his sole activity since his discharge from the army. Then one day the following strange conversation started suddenly between Sofia and Gioconda (that was the shopkeeper's name). The street was so narrow—really an alley—that they could converse from one shop to another without even having to move their chairs.

"It's not so warm anymore, Signora Gioconda," Sofia began. "I'm already wearing my shawl."

"It's almost winter," Gioconda answered with a mischievous smile that seemed almost insulting to Sofia. Nevertheless, it was clear that she too was quite pleased to be having the conversation and would not let it drop so easily. "Don't you like winter, Signora Vita?"

"Every season has its advantages and disadvantages. I have no complaints about any of them. But you must be happy that it will be getting cold. People will need warm clothes and a business like yours will pick up."

"Yours too, dear signora."

"Only so-so. People only want to buy new things now. They don't want to know about secondhand goods even though they cost less and last longer than the things they're making today."

"But now you have your brother to help you. He must be a great help to you, that boy."

To tell the truth, Sofia blushed a little at this point. But she had—as we said—a definite plan, even though she didn't want to admit it too clearly. So the conversation went on like this.

"Yes, my brother is a good boy."

"Wasn't he a watchmaker?"

"Yes, before he became a soldier."

"Is it true that he volunteered to serve?"

"Absolutely. For love of his country."

"He must have been discharged as an officer."

"Yes, of course."

"With what rank?"

"I don't know. I never asked him," Sofia lied.

Signora Gioconda understood that her neighbor didn't want to go any deeper into the subject of rank. And anyway, it didn't matter very much to her what rank her suitor had reached in the army.

"My shop is too small," Sofia went on, "there's no room for another soul in it. And we don't really need anyone else. My husband, myself, and the shop boy are enough. I would be very happy if I could find some other place to settle him."

"Why don't you let the boy go and take in your brother instead?"

"I can't do that. I'm very pleased with that boy. I haven't got the heart to let him go."

"We, on the other hand, are very unhappy with ours. It would be a great pleasure to change him."

There was a moment of silent embarrassment for both women that

Sofia forced herself to break. When it came to members of the family, this almost timid woman of ordinary intelligence was able to raise herself to the height of a Cavour, who flung the little province of Piedmont into the Crimean War.

"Do you want me to talk to Giuseppe about it?" she asked. "I think," and here Sofia lowered her eyes, "that he would be agreeable."

"My husband would be agreeable too," said the shopkeeper quickly, without lowering her eyes, which, in fact, were glittering strangely.

"Then you talk to him about it this evening. Meanwhile, I'll find out what my brother thinks. Ah, here he comes now."

In fact Giuseppe, taking long strides, was just coming out of a narrow side street. He greeted Signora Gioconda by raising his hat with a great flourish, then his sister more simply. Sofia hadn't yet told him that his brother-in-law had forbidden his visits to the shop; she always lacked the courage to do so, and besides, it would have interfered with her plan. Giuseppe took a chair from inside the store and placed it next to Sofia's. It was Friday night, nearly closing time. At any minute now, Sofia was expecting the shop assistant to return from an errand and her husband to arrive to accompany her to the synagogue as he did every evening, and particularly on holy days. She wasn't happy about Leone finding her brother in the shop, but didn't know how to get rid of him. Meanwhile Giuseppe was telling the shopkeeper that he had received a letter that day from his captain. As evidence of the high regard the captain had for Giuseppe, since meeting him in the army, he was offering him a position as secretary to Francesco Domenico Guerrazzi, a position, however, that Giuseppe had already decided to decline. The shopkeeper was listening to him with a steady smile while her eyes flashed as boldly as a pair of tavern lights. Finally Sofia, in the timid voice of a child asking a favor that she knows will be difficult to obtain, got up from her seat and, whispering as close as possible into Giuseppe's ear, asked him if by chance there was someplace else he could go. In that case she would give him money for cigarettes.

"How much will you give me?" he answered in the manner of a man not disposed to sell himself cheaply.

"How much? Ten soldi."

"Give me twenty, or else I'll stay. But don't let anyone see you."

Sofia walked toward the counter as if she were getting something.

And in fact she got two coins and left them on the counter in such a way, she thought, that only her brother would see them.

Giuseppe got up hurriedly, as if just at that moment he recalled an important engagement.

"Are you leaving already?" the shopkeeper asked with genuine regret. Her voice was trembling a little with anger, a little with that lust whose fame had overrun the (by now only symbolic) bounds of the ghetto and provided material for more issues of a tabloid that featured cartoons.

Giuseppe was preparing a soothingly chivalrous answer but had not yet taken the coins from the counter, when his sister Stella arrived on old Leone's arm. Together they looked like an ancient Oriental prince accompanied by a young and very beautiful slave girl. Sofia got up quickly to go to meet her husband, while Giuseppe hurried to pocket the money. He was hoping that his brother-in-law hadn't seen him. But the latter, despite his age and nearsightedness, had perfect vision for anything that had to do with his money. He was endowed with a kind of hypersensitivity to it; he could sense it being spent or moving around, even when it was no longer in his pockets. Therefore, he responded quite coolly to his wife's greetings and endearments and pretended not to be aware of Giuseppe's presence. The little shopkeeper continued smiling. Perhaps that smile, like the ink cuttlefish emit when they want to escape an enemy, was her only defense.

"Why don't you say something, Giuseppe?" asked the youngish Stella, whose tact at difficult moments didn't match the level of her beauty. "Are you in love, or something?"

Giuseppe broke into a loud laugh and hurried away after saying goodbye to the little shopkeeper and staring at her as if he wanted to hypnotize her. The following week he began working for her and immediately became as industrious and enterprising as if he were not an employee, but working on his own behalf. He learned, in short, not only how to sell but also (something much more difficult) how to buy. Thus, now that he no longer needed it, Giuseppe rewon the respect of his brother-in-law, who gladly admitted that he had been very wrong about the young man.

Doing Good

THE FAMILY WAS JUST RECOVERING from the terrors of unemployment, when one day at the table the father shot a thunderbolt into the newly blue sky—these few words that could easily have gotten him tried for uxoricide.

"Listen Anna," he said, "if by Friday I don't get my hands on two hundred florins, I'll lose my job and go to prison." And he confessed to his silent, terrified wife that he had spent the money he'd collected for his employer from a shopkeeper on the Via Molin Grande. He'd spent everything except ten florins still in his pocket. For the moment he'd been able to hide the shortage by saying that the shopkeeper hadn't had enough in the bank and had asked him to come back the following Friday. His employer, who had complete faith in his new collector—he had been recommended by someone far above mere respectability—had believed him without even asking to see the back accounts. He had also given him until next Friday. But now, in only three days, the time would be up and there was no doubt everything would be discovered. "It's possible," he added, "that out of consideration for your brother, Signor Almagià won't turn me in, but there's no doubt that the minute he finds out he'll fire me."

Having said this, he took a large, grimy wallet (a genuine bill collector's wallet) from an inside pocket of his jacket, extracted a ten-florin note and placed it on the table. "Here," he said, "it's better if you hold on to it. You've got your brother Augusto, you've got other rich relatives, and it won't be hard for you to get them to lend you two miserable hundreds. And you," he turned to the children, as if only just aware of his imprudence, "watch that you don't let a word of this out to anyone. If not—," and here he showed them the back of his large hand, as any good strict and proper father does when he threatens his children with a vigorous correction to the face. All four of them (two boys and two girls), who, since the beginning of the scene had stopped eating and were looking from their father to their mother, from executioner to victim, rose from their seats all together and ran crying to their mother's side, who, good housewife that she was, was standing at the side of the table ready to serve her family.

Recovering from the shock of the totally unexpected blow, Anna, who knew her husband to be irresponsible and a drinker, but never a thief, was about to call down curses upon him, when he, without finishing his food, got up, took his beat-up hat, slapped it down lower on his face than usual, and slamming the door behind him, left without another word. When Anna called him back from the doorway and then from the window, there was already more pain than menace in her voice, but the brute didn't even turn around. Clearly, he wanted to avoid a scene, escape the womanly whining that would do nothing but provoke him further. Not even the law, for that matter, punishes a criminal for his attempt to escape chastisement; a man who flees punishes himself.

Anna or Annuccia, as everyone in her family called her, except her husband who disliked endearments, was Jewish. She belonged to and declared herself proud of that religion which Heine says is not a religion, but a destiny. Whether the great German poet's *boutade* is true or false, Annuccia would have already ennobled that destiny with a heroic resignation to affliction and a sweetness of spirit that allowed her to feel deeply for the sufferings of others, even when her own were such that they would have dulled anyone else's sensibilities. Despite her husband's drunkenness and vulgarity, the humble, downtrodden woman reemerged victorious daily from the hell in which she lived, with the appeasing smile born of a clear conscience and faith in God. Giacomo, her shameless husband, was also Jewish but lacked the physical and moral makeup that would reflect his origin. He had a habitual preference (almost inconceivable in a Jew) for the tavern over his home. An Austrian citizen, born in Trieste, he had fled home as a young boy to enlist and fight with Garibaldi's Red Shirts at Mentana. On his return he served five years in the Austrian navy (four as duty, one as punishment), but those were the periods of his life that he spoke of with the most pleasure. He had saved a man one cloudy night by jumping into the sea; and while still a boy in short pants, using only his bare hands, he had put out a fire whose smoke had sent a whole neighborhood of Jews into the street below. As a counterpart to his proven courage and indisputable valor, he had an insensitivity to his own and others' pain that brought a flush of indignation to his wife's prematurely faded cheeks, and a certain mean-spiritedness and impatience with the plaints and problems to which the chosen people often abandoned themselves. Tall, thin, and very slender, Giacomo was like a green cane without vital sap. Annuccia was in every way his opposite—short, almost penguin-shaped, notwithstanding the troubles and privations of poverty. These had affected her (may God forgive me the comparison) like the flat of the blade upon cutlets of rare succulence, which gain in tenderness and flavor with every blow.

Alone and without any possibility of venting her anger on the guilty man she wouldn't see again until evening, Annuccia gave herself over to a violent and truly Jewish kind of despair. "Mamma, Mamma dear." Terrified and helpless, unable to escape her outbursts, the children implored Annuccia, as she recalled the cruel words which heralded the imminent return of that poverty, the mere memory of which still kept her awake at night. She walked back and forth in the kitchen, crying every once in a while, beating her fists against her head and chest. "Murderer, murderer, jailbird," she shouted at Giacomo, although he couldn't hear her. But the children could, and they were by now shrieking so loudly that the whole neighborhood heard them. This was the greatest affliction of Annuccia's life, because this time poverty would be accompanied by disgrace; and the wealthy relatives disgraced along with Giacomo (whom she had married against their wishes) would refuse her any help, even the comfort of words. They wouldn't even offer her the cup of coffee or the small glass of Florio marsala they always insisted she take even when, with aching heart and trembling from head to toe, the unhappy woman had just asked for money again. That small offering was an infinite comfort to her spirit; as if she were no longer poor Annuccia, but a cherished member of the family, or at least an ordinary visitor.

Two hundred florins! Where will I find two hundred florins? With the thought fixed in her head, the unhappy woman paced the kitchen like a wild beast surrounded by flames. "Hush, Mamma. Calm down," the oldest child, little Matilda, nearly twelve, Annuccia's only joy and the only help she had at home, pleaded uselessly. "How many times, Mamma, have you worried for nothing?" And the girl tried to calm Annuccia, get her to sit down, and to silence her little brothers and sisters, who, after the word *prison* escaped their father's mouth, had fallen into one of those irrational terrors all of us suffer to some degree in infancy. They were imagining damp, subterranean horrors, full of loathsome beasts, into which armed men would drag them at any moment, along with their mother and father. They weren't, as you can see, so far off the mark, although their primitive fantasies gave prison an aspect of earlier times.

"Tomorrow, you'll go see Uncle Augusto; he'll help you again, you'll see," the young solacer, good as she was lovely, went on.

"Maybe I should go right now," said Annuccia. "I can't live with these thoughts until tomorrow."

"Whatever you want, Mamma," Matilda was about to reply but couldn't because someone was knocking at the door.

"Who can it be?" asked the mother, who at that moment certainly didn't need company. Matilda ran to open the door.

It was the neighbor, who, frightened or attracted by the sound of weeping and furniture being moved, had come—so she said—to see if anyone was ill; or, so Annuccia instantly thought, to satisfy her curiosity. She didn't like the woman, not merely because she was a "goy," but because she knew her (or believed her) to be nosy and gossipy. Still, she recalled that when her family was hungry, the woman had spontaneously lent her a small sum of money that Annuccia hadn't yet given back and that the neighbor had never asked for. This recollection and her sense of obligation impelled Annuccia not only to let the woman in but to tell her of Giacomo's latest exploit despite Matilda's pleading looks. The neighbor listened, disapproved of Giacomo's behavior, but not with overly bitter words (a sensitivity for which Annuccia was grateful), commiserated with her friend, and left precipitously, as though distracted, promising she would return the next day. As soon as she was gone, Annuccia, already sorry that she had confided in that gossip and offended at her sudden departure, ran around the house knocking on wood.

"It was wrong to tell her," Matilda said immediately.

"Mind your own business," Annuccia answered resentfully. "And don't give your mother advice."

Matilda, who in reality was still a child and was at that moment wiping the youngest's snotty nose, grimaced, and her eyes filled with tears.

"You're crying?" Annuccia shouted and rushed at her almost as if she wanted to hit her. But suddenly she pulled her close, hugging her tightly, and thus united, the two wept for a long time.

When Matilda freed herself from the embrace that was the sweetest, most desired reward she could have, she told Annuccia, "You're right, Mamma. It's better for you to go see Uncle Augusto right away. After lunch today, I have only penmanship and gymnastics. I won't lose much not going back to school. I'll stay home and get the children's dinner. That way you can take as long as you want to without worrying about anything. I'll stay right here in the kitchen and not move an inch from the children."

Uncle Augusto, one of the leaders of the Jewish community, as well as a physician for Lloyd's Austria and for the Israelite Brotherhood of Charity, to whom Annuccia—as usual and like everyone else—applied for help, wasn't home when she asked the servant for him. Annuccia would have preferred having an arm cut off to requesting money from him again and was ready to leave, saying she would return the following day, when she heard Uncle Edoardo calling her. Almost ninety years old, Edoardo had been living for thirty years (or so he believed) on the interest of a small nest egg that would barely have been enough to pay the rent of a modest furnished room, completely cared for in the home of his nephew, not without accusing the nephew to those relatives who used to visit him and among whom he enjoyed an indisputable reputation for piety of "wrejecting" him (age had gone off with his "r's") yes, of "wrejecting" him and "wruining," his life. Annuccia found him stretched out on a huge deck chair with the inevitable red fez on his head, which for old Jews like him was almost a distinguishing mark. He was moaning about his debility and fear of death, complaints that came more from his lips than from his heart, especially when he sensed the approach of people who might comfort him for his ills, which were truly unending and worthy of pity. While still at the door of the house, Annuccia heard him exclaim as he always did, with those "w"s for "r"s, "God, if You're 'weally' there, help me die. If You're 'weally' there, help me die."

Having asked him one day if he, who was so pious and so deeply attached to his religion, didn't think it was a great sin to doubt the existence of God out loud, the old man turned his worn face to her, and with eyes full of a terrifying weariness and a flash of anger that made her tremble, answered. "Even the 'pwophets,'" he'd said, "even the 'pwophets' doubted."

"How are you, Uncle Edoardo," his niece asked, kissing him on his forehead. And hearing his answer delivered in a voice full of fury, sat next to him, adjusted the pillows in back of his head, listened patiently to his complaints, commiserated with him for his aches and pain, got up to open a window, "but not too much and not too little, just wright," remonstrated loudly with him against his enemies and the enemies of the Jewish people; and finally with great embarrassment and remorse to be speaking of her own troubles in the presence of others which seemed so much worse, she told him of her husband's new villainy and the threat that hung over her family so recently restored to security.

"Great news," said the pious old man. "Great news you've brought me." ("Great" as usual had sounded like "gwate.") "You didn't have to come, if you didn't have anything better to say to a poor old man."

"I know, dear Edoardo, that you are a saint and that you love me," said Annuccia, convinced that her uncle felt her pain, and changing his crudely egotistical words into proof of affection and paternal tenderness. "I came to talk about it with my dear brother Augusto, not with you, Uncle, but after seeing you, you know how we women are, we always need to let our troubles out." And her eyes, which were still red from all her crying, filled with tears again.

"And why do you want to talk to your brother Augusto?"

"Naturally, it's not a matter of a gift," said Annuccia quietly, moving her seat closer to her uncle's; and after convincing herself that the servant couldn't hear her, went on, "It's just a simple loan that I'll repay so much every month out of Giacomo's salary. So, Edoardo dear, you who are so good, you have to do me a real favor."

"I don't have any money," the pious old man interrupted.

"I know, I know you don't have any," said Annuccia, placing her hand, gloved in black cotton, on her uncle's stiff, hairy one. "But I live so far away and I can't come back before tomorrow because of the children. What I would really like is for you to talk to my brother for me. Just one word from you . . ."

"I don't appwrove of bothering poor Augusto every day. Do what I say. Take my advice for once. Let that good-for-nothing husband of yours go to jail. He's a robber." (Of course, the word had come out "wobber.") "I would never have believed it of a Jew."

"He isn't bad," said Annuccia, who had gotten up to reassure herself that the door was really closed and that no one was listening behind it. "He isn't bad. He's just irresponsible. When he does something wrong, he's the first to suffer. Even today he gave me ten florins that were left from the—the receipts. If he were really bad, he would have spent them too."

"And how did he spend it?"

It was strange. Annuccia hadn't yet asked herself how her husband had managed to spend a hundred and ninety florins in a few days. She thought of many things, one after the other, one contradicting the other; till finally she remembered that in the depths of their poverty Giacomo had borrowed to go drinking. She explained to her uncle.

"Jail, jail. That's where 'wobbers' belong," the furious old moralist shouted.

"And what about us?" Annuccia asked timidly.

"You should never have married him. Did I ever 'mawwy'?" the old man asked. "Your Uncle Edoardo was always telling you he wasn't the man for you."

"That's true, Annuccia sighed, "but who can say that God didn't want me near him to save him? What would have become of him without me?"

"I've always helped everyone," the slurring went on, "even my enemies. Once upon a time, a poor soul followed me from the slaughterhouse to the temple square, and instead of calling a policeman, or just giving him money which, like your husband, he would have spent on drink, I took him to a bakery and bought him a piece of bread as big as this."

"I believe you, Edoardo dear. I believe you."

"And another time, a man who was disloyal to me in business, yes ma'am, disloyal, was walking in front of my store when he fell to the ground in a convulsion. What do you think your uncle Edoardo did then? Uncle Edoardo, who no one cares about? I didn't just sit there laughing at my enemy. No, I myself brought him a glass of water with these very hands, without first asking if he was a Christian or a Jew. This is what your uncle Edoardo did and much more too. But one has to do good, not talk about it. Your right hand mustn't know what your left hand is doing." Edoardo's speech impediment had not impeded his fervor. "Do me a favor, Annuccia. Give me that little packet on the table."

"The sugar?"

"The sugar." The old man, who had great faith in its nutritive powers, ate it constantly.

Annuccia listened to him for some time longer, comforted him as best she could, considering her own state of mind. Then she got up to leave.

"You'll talk to my brother about it?" she asked.

"Yes, I'll talk to him even though it goes against my conscience and morality to help a 'wobber.' I'll do it for your sake."

And in fact, the following day Annuccia received a letter from her brother Augusto that she opened with foreboding. The letter read,

"My dear Annuccia. Uncle Edoardo told me of the fine act your husband committed against you, against your children, and against the decent man to whom I myself had recommended him. I am sorry, but I cannot give you what you ask of me, because it would do you harm, not good."

"It's clear," little Matilda, wise beyond her age, in whose presence Annuccia was reading with trembling hands and voice, interrupted. "It's clear what that sainted Uncle Edoardo was up to."

"I can, however, give you two hundred florins personally and get the community to give you more, in addition to an annual subsidy on the promise that you use the money to open a kosher delicatessen, which we haven't had here in town, since Signora Goldschmidt's death. The work is easy and the income certain, so much so that we have already had twenty applications. But I am reserving this benefice for you, my beloved and unhappy sister, on the sole condition that you get a divorce immediately, or in some other way separate permanently from Giacomo, who has given you nothing but sorrow and who could—may God forbid it—be the death of you. Come see me tomorrow at two with the proper answer. It's the only thing that you can do and the only thing I advise you to do for your own good. Your affectionate brother, Augusto."

"Are you going to do it, Mamma?" Matilda asked, seeing Annuccia silent, with her face set almost in a grimace of anger.

"My brother Augusto," she answered finally, "is a decent man with a heart of gold; but I never thought that he would advise me to leave my husband. Giacomo will be what he wants to be, even a thief (the word was more intuited by Matilda than spoken by her mother), but I won't leave him as long as I live." And having said these words, she tore the letter into tiny pieces so that Giacomo wouldn't be able to read it when he came back; then, as an extra precaution, she threw the pieces into the fire. Because Annuccia was perhaps the "woman of valor" of whom the scriptures say, "She does good and not evil for him, all the days of her life."

There were two days left to the time Giacomo had fixed, and by now Annuccia, as a last resort, was prepared to go see his employer, throw herself at his feet and tell him the whole story, when Divine Providence— which never deserts those who believe in it—arrived in dirty, sloppy clothes, out of a pocket hidden under the skirts of the Catholic neighbor so often justly criticized for her nosiness and mean tongue that one of Annuccia's torments was remorse for the guilty ease with which she had confided in that gossip. Without anyone having urged her, without a word from any of them, she drew out of that pocket and set out, one on top of the other, twenty banknotes of ten florins each, or rather twenty angels from Paradise. She didn't want a receipt. She agreed to a slow but regular monthly repayment because she, too, she said, wasn't rich and had other people to take care of. Who can describe the astonishment, confusion, gratitude, and happiness of Annuccia, who had already thought herself beyond hope, to see her family saved from poverty and dishonor by the person she least thought capable of it? It was all she could do not to kneel before her, and in the consternation of the moment, she could think of no other way to thank her for her kindness than to confess all the evil that she had so unjustly thought of her. "How much," she concluded, looking at her savior, her eyes brilliant with tears, "how much one needs to wait before judging a person! I now owe you my life, two hundred florins, plus ten from before; and I will give them back to you on time, even if my children and I have to go without food."

The following day, when Giacomo came home for dinner, his wife, who hadn't spoken a word to him since the day of his confession, said, "You'll have the two hundred florins tomorrow to give back to Signor Almagià." And she watched his face to see the impression those liberating words would have on a man she imagined was being devoured by remorse and fear.

"What two hundred florins?" Giacomo said, without looking up from the plate.

"What do you mean, what?" exclaimed Annuccia. "Didn't you say . . . ?"

"Oh, that," Giacomo said calmly. "I forgot to tell you that evening, that after I left here I settled the whole thing on the spot. I got the money and repaid it. And you can keep those ten florins that were left over as a present."

Annuccia took a knife from the table and plunged it into her husband's chest, just over the heart. The impulse was so strong, the temptation so powerful, that for a moment she almost believed she had committed the act. But all she did was to say, or rather stammer, the following words, sounding as stunned as if she had just revived from a faint, "You forgot . . . forgot to tell me? You could forget such a thing? And let me go around thinking it for a week?"

Giacomo shrugged his shoulders. Then he told her to go right out and buy him a plain suitcase, and to pack some underwear and his new suit in it. He had to make the ten o'clock ship for Spalato the following morning.

"To do what?" asked his wife once more overcome with terror. She vaguely remembered having heard that in Spalato, where she had lived for a while as a child and where she still had relatives, there had recently been an outbreak of smallpox.

"I'm going to nurse people with the pox," Giacomo answered. "They're giving me twelve florins a day in addition to food and lodging. Elio Treves from the hospital, who'd been asked to find suitable people, came looking for me himself to tell me about it. It seems that down there no one has the guts to do it. I accepted on the condition that they advance me two hundred florins without which I couldn't leave your Signor Almagià, and that they send you my pay, old girl, minus a deduction for the loan. The tips will be enough for me. I hear they're good. If I need anything I'll write."

"You're not going," his wife shouted. And she threw herself around his neck, trying to kiss him despite the strong odor of bad wine that came from his mouth.

Giacomo pushed her away. "Get out of here, old lady, before I knock you senseless," he said. But in my dialect these words (which the reader can easily interpret himself) can even have an affectionate meaning.

Seven Stories

1912–1913

Valeriano Rode

MADDALENA FERRANDI RODE, a woman of forty-five, was pregnant for the fourth time. Six months of worrying about this unexpected, or as its victim thought of it, unwarranted, pregnancy, had not been enough to overcome her dread of it. At her age, with a husband twelve years older than she, in a city such as Trieste in the summer of 1911, when the threat of inflation was more terrifying to its inhabitants than the denials of an outbreak of cholera, pregnancy was undoubtedly a misfortune which even women in better spiritual and material circumstances than Maddalena had trouble accepting. What would become of her children, all of them still babies, of her unborn child, and of her husband, the secretary of a company dealing in citrus fruits, whose energies (strange to say in a man of his temperament) had deteriorated to the point that he was suffering from nervous fatigue, with so many and such troubling symptoms that he hadn't yet consulted a doctor, more out of fear than economy. God had truly abandoned her, punished her for others' sins with this new life, whose stirrings under better circumstances she, a woman made for birth and nursing, would have felt if not as a blessing, at least as a necessity to be faced without displeasure or fear.

The poor soul, exhausted by these thoughts and her many daily chores, was sitting before a wide-open window at a sewing machine she had just stopped using, with her eyes fixed before her and her arms folded in a pose that vaguely recalled the great Napoleon contemplating a painting of Moscow in flames. From the picturesque Grand Canal, which the windows of her tiny apartment faced, and on which ships from Bari and Chioggia with their summer cargo of watermelons and such were moored, there rose, along with the shouts of the street vendors, the stench of rotten fruit floating on the stagnant water. But instead of sickening her, that smell, which seemed an external statement of her internal torment, pleased Maddalena more than the perfume of flowers would have done.

So this was Maddalena's state of mind when her servant entered the room to prepare for dinner. Maria set the table for only two—for Maddalena and her husband. One of the old man's latest quirks, perhaps the one that most alienated his wife from him, was that he no longer wanted the children at the table. And it had happened abruptly, from one evening to the next, when previously it had seemed Valeriano couldn't bear to eat without them. "When a Christian wants to go crazy, he ought to at least give you some notice," is how Maria reacted the first time she was ordered to have the children eat in the kitchen with her.

When her preparations were done, Maria took the newspaper, *La Piccola della Sera,* from the table and placed it in front of Maddalena on the Singer. But seeing that Maddalena, who generally read the paper every day, didn't even look at it, Maria decided she herself would give her employer the most interesting news.

"That American meat ship," she said, "they made it leave port without unloading. It's just as well."

The ship was the *Martha Washington,* an Austro-American steamer that had arrived the day before and had not been granted (because of a regulation of agricultural protectionism, in itself unjust) a permit to unload the huge tonnage of meat stored in its refrigerated hold. In spite of the fuss the opposition press raised about the outrage, the populace was so completely uninterested in long-dead meat, requiring lengthy and compli- cated cookery to make it edible, that it barely acknowledged the affair. And Maddalena, who couldn't have cared less about it, didn't answer.

"Do you want to try to have the children at the table tonight? I have a feeling your husband won't object. In fact, he'll even be happy to have them with him again."

"And start an argument?" Maddalena finally spoke.

What a swine, is what Maria, to whom ten years of uninterrupted service and a good bit of wages in arrears had conceded an anarchical freedom of speech, felt like saying. But seeing the look on Maddalena's face, she held back, and asked instead for money to get the egg phosphate, a medication all the children now had to take in various doses. The obsession with tonics was another of Valeriano's quirks. He, who would never have swallowed a spoonful of medicine at any price, had gotten the idea that his children, born of an old father and a mother no longer in her youth, could not possibly grow up healthy without ingesting the greatest possible quantities of up-to-date tonics. And he was inexorable on the subject, even at his own expense, depriving himself when necessary of the only luxuries in his life, his afterdinner cigar and the two-cent cigarettes he smoked at work.

But just that evening, Maddalena didn't have a penny. It was the last day of the month and she was waiting for her husband to bring home his salary, which for some time now he had been turning over to her in its entirety, and from which, almost like a mother doling out pennies to a child for sweets, she had been daily giving him loose change for tobacco. That particular month she was even hoping for a raise in his salary, something his employer certainly owed to an employee of long standing, particularly a family man, during an era when things were becoming more difficult every day. But what if he were let go instead? At the end of every month, between her hope for some slight amelioration of her situation and her fear of ultimate disaster, Maddalena was always in a state of anxiety. She told Maria she'd give her the money for the medicine later and the servant left the room with an air of dissatisfaction. Immediately thereafter, two short consecutive rings of the bell sounded. The old man was home.

Even before her husband entered the room, Maddalena knew from his footsteps that something unusual had happened or was about to happen. Valeriano Rode was a tall, thin old man with an aquiline nose and the short receding chin of the weak willed. The son of well-to-do parents, he had spent his youth in every kind of sport that accorded with his need for solitude. More than anything else, he was a great walker. He would often depart his home, just like that, the way others might go out for a walk of two hours, almost without telling anyone, carrying only a walking stick, and without any thought to his need for clean clothes. When those he was wearing became dirty, he'd either throw them away or give them away, and (it was far easier) buy new ones. When his parents died and his inheritance was gone, he had to make use of his knowledge of foreign languages (the only studies he'd ever enjoyed) and take a job as a secretary in a trading house, and perhaps he was content that the constraint freed him from a secret burden of fantasies and torments, which had become unbearable by then. If he was past his prime when he married Maddalena (who had had an unhappy love affair and was thirty-six at the time), it was partly due to chance (an ad, placed as a lark in a daily newspaper, to which Maddalena had, also as a lark, responded) and partly the result of one of those deep emotional upheavals that suddenly force human beings who have lived by their own rules to rejoin the flock and, as a kind of overreaction, to undertake responsibilities of a nature and degree that are more than they can bear. At any rate, after ten years of marriage this eccentric old man, who for a quarter of a century had been sitting in an office from morning till long past dark writing business letters by gaslight, could still, on the whole, pass for a retired sailor or army veteran (which perhaps he would have been in a more adventurous era). The disquieting nervous ailment, whose symptoms had been frightening Maddalena more out of concern for her children than out of affection for him, was still not apparent to outsiders. Valeriano's harsh whims were asserted at home, for it was only there that he could act out his tragic unhappiness. Perhaps his wasn't truly an illness so much as a crisis of old age, exacerbated by remorse about a life of failed hopes (though Valeriano himself couldn't have said what they were), and of that sudden rekindling of passions, which taken together with a weakening of the will, makes a man's passage from maturity to old age the time he is most dangerous to himself, as well as to others, and the most nettlesome of the stages of his life. Valeriano's problem first became apparent with that harsh detachment from his children, with that sudden rush of hatefulness for those to whom he had until then shown only love. Then there'd been that explosion of senile eroticism which sends so many men over the age of fifty to jail or to the hospital, and to which, in part, Maddalena owed her misfortune. But immediately afterward he distanced himself from his wife as he had from his children, and in the same harsh way. Even the late paternity didn't give him that small sense of pride that old men feel when they can display a pregnant wife of impeccable reputation. He now barely spoke to Maddalena, seemed to be afraid of her and to suspect her of thoughts that would never have entered her head. And as is always the case with emotional dramas, there were economic problems making matters worse.

Valeriano had recently taken to spending a goodly sum of money, though Maddalena did not know on what. It was so much money, that for a while she suspected the old man of having a lover. But looking through his pockets and drawers, all she found was a membership card in a boat club. She recalled then that in his youth Valeriano had won second prize in a regatta. Was it possible—oh, Lord—that a man of nearly sixty could be seriously thinking of resuming the activities of his youth? But Valeriano would come home every evening after work at the same time, and therefore hadn't ever made use of his membership. And that of course was the case. As Maddalena suspected from the moment she found the card, this peculiarity was merely another indication of her husband's madness, a last desperate attempt by Valeriano to return to his self of forty years earlier. Just as stagnant waters give rise to glowing phosphorescence, in his early state of mental disorganization, Valeriano was subject to strange and vivid flashes (especially after a meal or just before falling asleep) that suddenly recreated thoughts, places, people, fragments of landscape, snatches of conversation, even recollections from his "globe-trotter" days, totally unrelated to the rest of his thoughts. And he recalled all of it in the most minute detail, with a precise sense of the time, almost with the smell of the air and all his surroundings—febrile visions, which like drum rolls reawakened the torment of his impotent regrets. But why impotent? Because healthy and robust as he assured himself he was, wouldn't he, if he had no family, be able to make up in his old age for the time he'd wasted growing moldy at his writing table? Return to what he had been? Visit new countries—one above all, Dalmatia, whose beautiful coastline he'd seen in Lloyd of Austria advertisements, and which had particularly attracted him? To tour it in small stages, then go beyond it to the Balkans, the Orient. But what about money? Oh, if only he had put aside for himself all that he'd spent on his wife and children for the past ten miserable years. How different his old age would be! Perhaps the best time of his life. Why had he ever married? Why had he produced these three, soon to be four, mouths that fed on his ten hours of daily labor? Wasn't it unjust that man had to suffer his entire life for the consequences of an act committed to satisfy a need of the senses, which nature then turned to an end he didn't desire? Fatherhood. What's fatherhood, anyway? It's as if someone eating fruit casually tosses a seed out the window, and a tree happens to grow from it. What obligation is the man under to spend the most precious hours of his day dealing with that tree? To water it, to trim it, to make it grow with the sweat of his own labor? And all this even if he doesn't like the tree, or if he'd wanted something completely different in its place? Now that Valeriano no longer loved his children, now that he admitted to himself that he had never loved them despite his obsession with tonics, or at least that he hadn't loved them with the passionate and jealous love of other fathers, it seemed monstrous to him, inconceivable, that as the result of one act these creatures had been born to perpetuate life's wrongs. To his disturbed mind, the relationship between cause and effect, which is so clear to the rest of the world, became confused and fragmented, and the abomination of his entrapment drove him to desperation. Out of it grew a personality particularly antagonistic to him, with whom he would have interminable discussions while coming from and going to work, and which he destroyed by a last fatal question without answer, only to revive it to offer it yet another proof of betrayal. A horse, an almost skeletal horse, which regularly would walk the street beside him for a while every evening, and which was always drawing a load greater than it could bear, with no advantage to the poor creature bearing all that weight, seemed to him the true symbol of a father of a family: the characteristic symbol. And he would have given anything, would have done anything in his power to stop resembling that horse. So it was that one evening Maddalena heard him give that vile order that the children eat in the kitchen with the servant. The sight of their pale, young faces, of their lips that were too colorless or too red despite the expense of the tonics, irritated him as instant living proof of his entrapment. Then he was overcome by a feeling beyond the eroticism of old age, by a kind of anguish, a tenderness, a need to reconcile himself to life, to be like everyone else. And Maddalena became pregnant. But from that moment on, it was all over. He would have left his family, would have traveled through Dalmatia, or wherever, with or without remorse (it was now only an insignificant detail), if only he had a little money for bread and shoes. But how to get even that minimum? To insure himself of at least a year, that much time, after which he would either go under or find something to do where no one, particularly his family, knew him? His employer's trust in Valeriano was so certain and secure that many times when the employer traveled, he would leave the keys to his strongbox with his old employee. Even so? What if he had him arrested? But no. That coward would never have the courage to denounce him. He might even be happy to be rid of a sixty-year-old man for a mere few thousand crowns. He'd already set a very young and very enthusiastic boy to work beside him, a German barely out of adolescence, who didn't even smoke during work, as, he said, all his compatriots did. What was worse, in the state Valeriano was in, solitude and the company of prisoners seemed preferable to him. But it turned out there was no need for him to steal or to go to prison. That last evening in August, when Maddalena, on hearing her husband approach, sensed that something had happened, Valeriano had been called in by his employer, warmly thanked for his long and faithful service, and had been let go with—and this was a nonobligatory act of generosity—recompense of twenty-four hundred crowns, a year's pay. Too little to live on, but to Valeriano at that moment, almost too much. It meant victory.

"So, are you going to tell me what happened?" Maddalena asked, seeing a fork tremble in the old man's hands.

"Nothing," Valeriano answered, as his courage ebbed. But immediately afterward, responding to one of those inner thrusts that ten years earlier had propelled him into marriage, he said simply, "I'm leaving." And the wretched woman's eyes, the color of air, opened wide.

"Leaving? Where are you going?"

"I don't know yet. But I'm leaving. I've decided."

Maddalena felt as if she were going to faint, but immediately guessed a part of the truth. "Signor Wilda let you go?"

"Yes, just now, this evening. But it isn't that."

"I was expecting this," Maddalena said, and her voice seemed to come from someone else, someone far away. Then a last hope gave her the strength to resume the terrible dialogue.

"And why are you leaving? Have you found work elsewhere?"

"No. But even if I did, it wouldn't matter. I'm leaving because I'm leaving. To get away from you. This is the last time we'll eat together."

Maddalena jumped to her feet as if her husband had been struck by apoplexy. Without thinking she put her hand on his forehead to see if he had fever. It's finally happened, she thought, remembering that Valeriano's father and an uncle who'd been a priest had died in the madhouse.

Valeriano stood up too, but slowly. Though there was still an innocent expression on his face, his hands were shaking and large beads of sweat covered his forehead. As he reached for his handkerchief to dry his brow, the money hidden in his jacket pocket scattered to the floor.

"What's all this money?" Maddalena asked, bending quickly to gather it.

"My severance pay."

Maddalena couldn't help counting the money, then smiled bitterly with quivering lips as if she were speaking or praying to herself.

"Give it to me. It's mine," said Valeriano.

Silently, she handed him the money. But so great was her agitation that there were moments when she felt she was passing out, or that she would soon need help and not be able to call for it.

"There's twenty-four hundred crowns there," Valeriano began again in a voice that could have been saying a million. "We'll divide it in half, twelve hundred for me, twelve hundred for you, all right?" And putting half the money down on the table, he picked up his hat and walking stick as if he'd just given his wife food money and were going out for a cup of coffee or a shave.

Maddalena moved toward her husband, placing herself firmly between him and the door.

"You're sick," she said with an unexpected sweetness that startled Valeriano. Then she set a plate on the money as a paperweight and pulled over a chair. "Sit down, dear," she said. "Sit down and let's talk about this."

The tone of his wife's voice was so compelling that Valeriano suddenly felt he had to obey her. Maddalena remained standing in front of him, with her large belly in full view. Flies were buzzing around the dishes in which their dinner was getting cold.

"Why don't you tell me where you want to go?" Maddalena asked, still in that sweet manner.

"Because I don't know yet," Valeriano answered timidly. "And then, as I said, it won't make any difference."

He's definitely crazy, thought Maddalena. And at one and the same time, she felt both a certain compassion for him and a desire to grab him by the throat and throttle him. Nevertheless, she controlled herself, remembering having heard it said that you don't deal with crazy people head on. "And you think," she said, "this is the moment to abandon me?"

Valeriano didn't answer. There was a long silence.

"All right. If you've decided to go, go. But not right now. Not tonight. At least wait until I can pack a suitcase for you." And saying that, she felt certain of being able to restrain him until she could see what course things would take, and decide how to proceed after that.

"What's there to pack?"

"Don't you want to take your new suit and some clean linen, so you'll be able to change? Do you want to go with just the shirt on your back? And when it gets dirty?"

"I'll buy a new one."

"And when you've spent all the money?"

Valeriano didn't answer.

"And you don't care about me? About how you're leaving me?"

"It's not my problem."

"And your children? Who will provide for your children? And for the one I'm carrying?" And she beat her hands against her belly, as if to crush something evil.

The father stretched his arms in a wide gesture, as priests in the pulpit do when they want to beckon Divine Providence. Perhaps for the first time, it occurred to Maddalena that her husband wasn't a madman, but a monster. And once more she felt a desire to throw herself at him.

"You're right too," Valeriano said finally, almost to himself, "but I . . . I don't want to . . . I don't have to be like that horse anymore."

"Like what horse?" asked Maddalena, who felt a sudden chill down her spine, the kind she'd felt when, as a terrified child getting out of bed in the dark, she imagined a cold and hairy hand about to seize her. She no longer had any doubt. Her husband was crazy. But Valeriano, on the other hand, was thinking of how wonderful it was that he would never, in all his comings and goings, have to see that dreadful symbol of his life again.

"You think I'm crazy, or acting like a child," he said, "but you're wrong. I'm neither."

Maddalena sank into a chair, sobbing, defeated, without, however, losing sight of her husband, and certain she would soon have to call for help.

"I'm just a poor man who wants to do at last what my heart has been telling me to do for a long time. Maybe it's late, but better late than never."

Maddalena was still crying. And it seemed as though the old man's courage was growing with his victim's convulsive sobs.

"I made a mistake to get married, I know it. I'm not the kind of man to have a family. But what better way is there to correct the mistake now, than what I am doing?" And he walked toward the door.

"Maria," Maddalena called, but in a voice that the servant would barely hear.

Valeriano opened the door. The noise the children were making in the kitchen reached him. One of them was crying.

"Is it my fault these miserable kids were born? Did we intend to have a family? No. So?" And he stopped, almost as if he were awaiting an answer on which his life depended. In that last moment it seemed as if his wife had become for him the personification of that enemy with whom, coming and going to work, he'd had those long discussions. But as there was no response either from her or from himself, Valeriano bowed his head, sighed, and vanished without looking back.

Maddalena managed to stand up again and to call Maria once more. The servant was coming into the room just at that moment to ask where the old man could possibly have gone with that look on his face, and without answering the children who were calling him.

"My husband is mad," Maddalena said suddenly and firmly. "We have to run after him and stop him."

A Man

WHEN THE PAINTER SCIPIO RATTA returned from a two-month trip, he found that Maria, with whom he lived as man and wife though they were not married, had changed a great deal. He felt that her affection was no longer that of a lover, but of a mother or sister. And, as he had the intuition of a consummate neurasthenic, one day after lunch, while Maria was getting dressed to go out, he told her in his ordinary voice, the deep, uninflected voice of a man tragically focused on himself, what he was thinking. "You're in love with Nardi." Nardi was another painter, an acquaintance of Scipio's.

"Yes," Maria answered, discovering within herself at that terrible moment the courage of truth, something women can locate (though not always) when they sense their preferred weapons will be useless.

Scipio felt as if he'd been struck in the center of his chest, but said nothing. He barely wrinkled his brow and bent his large, heavy head. It seemed to Maria that she heard a sigh, almost a groan.

"Forgive me," she said, moving closer to him, trying—shockingly—to caress him.

But Scipio parried the attempt and went on still without any reaction, as though he were talking to himself.

"If you're in love with Nardi, go live with Nardi."

He'd experienced something like a brief mental lapse. Felt as if he had been out of his mind and that recovering now, it was an effort to recall who he was and where he was. In a few seconds, his entire life had changed, changed forever. But even in that moment of anguish that would surely bring him months and months of illness, if not immediate death, he had no doubt about what he had to do.

When it happens that a woman who is fundamentally honest dislikes a man because she's fallen in love with another, she leaves the house of the first and goes to live with the second. He didn't yet understand the perpetual childishness of women—the cause of their inability to exercise moral independence of any sort—and conceded to the woman he loved— God alone knew how dear she was to him—the right to do what he thought he would have done in her situation. The fault lay with the person left behind, with the one who wasn't more lovable.

Maria, who should have wanted that resolution, who in fact had sworn to Nardi that nothing else would make her as happy (if she didn't write to tell Scipio that, it was only because she was afraid of causing him too much suffering), felt on hearing these words tremendous disillusionment— not at all that sense of liberation she had expected. It seemed to her too sad a prospect, if not completely impossible, to separate from the man who had been her first lover and to whom she owed three years (and not the worst years) of her life. When a man thinks he has behaved generously in offering a poor woman such a clear decision, it only shows that he knows nothing about the weakness of the female heart and doesn't understand to what tortures his decision condemns the unhappy, guilty woman. Maria was now in love with Nardi (an intense, not at all trivial person), but that love didn't alter her affection for Scipio, who, in truth, was truly her husband. Just as a religious commitment often becomes more intense after a sin, so the affections of an adulterer are often revived, as though fertilized by remorse. This explains the letters full of enthusiastic affection that Maria wrote to Scipio while he was away, every evening on her return from visits to her lover, as well as the explosion of tears, the attempt to kiss his hand, and to hold on to him, now that she saw that he was ready to walk out and she understood that she was losing him forever. Why hadn't he killed her?

Even when Scipio received a letter from Maria saying that she had left the house (and the letter was full of anguish and blessings), he didn't go back there again. He made the sacrifice of paying the rest of the rent in one lump sum, and spent the extraordinarily long, blustery winter hidden in his studio like a hibernating animal. Except that his hibernation was not without suffering. It was like one of those agitated nights when the consciousness of the dreamer does nothing to change the terrifying nature of what is dreamed. He didn't feel hate for Maria, or even for his fortunate rival. What he did feel was a deep, unassailable dislike for himself. In the man whom the woman he loved had chosen, however, there could be nothing but the utmost virtue of body and soul. Thus even Nardi's paintings, which had never appealed to him, which he had described as superficial, with false pretensions to being revolutionary when they were essentially bourgeois, now seemed different to him, and he felt in his heart that he could have fooled himself. He visualized Nardi, with his youthful good looks, made to please women, and then his own self, small and rachitic, with his disproportionately large head, the unkempt beard that Maria had so often pleaded with him to trim, and his wide, rapturous eyes, which, when they were fixed on no matter what object—fabric, furniture, or animal—seemed not to be merely looking at it but adoring it. Scipio had "religious" eyes, Nardi brilliant ones. Young people and women are always attracted to eyes that shine. There was in his studio an enormous canvas, which, like all the others in it, was incomplete. In this painting, among a throng of people intent on watching an unseen happening, one figure, absorbed in a different vision, stood out from the rest—his own head as a saint, a large sketch for a potential masterpiece that Scipio had always cherished. Now he hated it. Hated seeing that part of himself, larger than life. And he turned the canvas to the wall as if it were a forbidden thing.

Instead, he studied a portrait of Maria, this too incomplete, in which the woman was portrayed seated, wearing a red-and-white-flowered dressing gown. He had begun it before leaving on his trip and now he dreamed of completing it (two or three sittings would be all he needed). Whereupon, placing that testimony to the tragedy that had befallen him as man and artist nearby, he took himself to bed to die, not of a physical ailment, nor by suicide, but of disaffection with life. How could he get a model now? Dreams, always dreams. It was a dream to think he might complete that portrait; a dream that he would die of anything but cancer or a heart attack; and even so, who knew when. It's the creaking gate that hangs longest.

Nevertheless, when winter finally ended and spring arrived with those first long, perfumed evenings in which only prisoners don't go out walking, Scipio remembered that he was not imprisoned, except by himself, and suddenly he began going out again. He took walks by himself in certain city streets that had special meaning only for him. Streets that he had known since childhood, the only time of his life he still thought of without despair. And so it was that one evening he saw Maria and Nardi across the way from him. His heart skipped a beat; then without thinking about what he was doing, without knowing exactly why, intuitively, just as if nothing had ever happened, he walked toward the two lovers. They, too, had seen him, or better still, had become aware of his presence, and had stopped for a moment to look into each other's eyes. Maria, suddenly startled, felt as if she would fall, and Nardi took her arm to hold her up and help her continue on. But Scipio was already upon them, just two steps away, standing there silently, as though entranced. Even in his own great confusion he noticed that Maria's eyes were reddish, the eyes of someone who cried a great deal. It was that detail that allowed him—who knows why!—to speak, and enabled him to understand his motive for having so unhesitatingly walked up to face the source of his misfortune.

"Good evening," he said, tipping his hat. And then he turned toward Maria, and in a soft, even-tempered voice said, "If you don't mind, I would like to ask you a favor."

"By all means," the woman answered, her imploring eyes turning from one man to the other. She had never believed that Scipio had really forgiven her and felt that whatever might happen now would be her fault.

"Oh, nothing serious," said Scipio, smiling, as if he were trying to reassure her. "You know the portrait of you that I began before my trip? Well, I'd like to finish it, that's all."

Maria looked at Nardi, who was frowning at her. No one spoke.

"Two or three sittings would be enough," Scipio resumed with the air of a timid child, in whose request others found something evil, though he himself knew it—or believed it—to be innocent.

"Would it be all right with you?" Maria finally asked her lover. And though her tone was meek, it seemed to say, Now we'll see if you're afraid.

"Why not?" Nardi asked. Perhaps he didn't want to appear inferior to Scipio, who not only introduced him to Maria as soon as he had expressed an interest in meeting her, but who even afterward never appeared to be afraid to leave the two of them alone together, and had never prevented them from seeing each other.

"I'll do it," said the woman then.

"Really?" Scipio exclaimed. "Oh, how grateful I'll be to you!" And suddenly he began speaking, not only without his previous sense of constraint, but with gaiety.

"Can we begin tomorrow?"

"Tomorrow," Maria answered, and she, too, no longer felt distrustful.

"Is three all right for you?"

Maria thought for a moment, then nodded her head.

"So, it's all set. Three at my studio. Or would you prefer it if I came to your place?" he added, speaking to Maria, but turning to Nardi. Nardi made a vague gesture as if to say it was all the same to him.

"In that case, I'm happier in my studio," Scipio went on, with increasing good cheer. "It's better not to change the background, and to tell the truth I don't think I could really work away from home." And he smiled.

Nardi smiled too, but in a different way. It was the smile of a man who was angry with himself.

"And if you don't mind," Scipio went on, "bring along that red-and-white-flowered gown of yours. Remember? It's what you're wearing in the portrait. Do you still have it?"

"I think so," Maria answered.

"I can only work a little at a time. I get tired very quickly," Scipio told Nardi. "I've been sick and the days are still short. I'd like Maria to be punctual, something that's not at all her nature. So I'd appreciate it, Nardi, if you saw to it that she gets to my studio on time."

"All right," Nardi assured him. And that particular smile of his became greatly intensified. But Scipio didn't notice.

"Thank you," he said again.

There followed a long, very distressing silence, in which the three of them stood around, unable to think of anything to say. It gave Scipio time to recover himself and feel frightened at what he had dared. He raised his hat quickly, said good-bye, and left, almost at a run. As if he were being chased.

How happy they were together! he said to himself, as soon as he was back at the studio where he was now living. And he remembered how much he had suffered because of his unfortunately small stature, next to Maria, who was tall and carried herself regally. But why were her eyes red? Was she unhappy? He felt that the thought was making him hate Nardi.

Maria was punctual and Scipio, animated by that exaltation which in him always preceded great exhausting crises, greeted her simply, but with the gaiety of a schoolboy. He had set a large fire in the dressing room next to the studio, but when Maria took off her coat, he saw that underneath it she was already dressed for the sitting. He also saw that she was trembling. He, however, was not the least bit uncomfortable.

"Do you want to sit?" And he pushed a chair over to where a white canvas was already prepared and set on an easel. He took up his brushes and palette and, without further ado, began painting.

"Aren't you going to finish my portrait?" asked Maria, surprised to see a blank canvas in place of the one Scipio had spoken to her about.

"No, I'm beginning another," he answered smiling. "Does that bother you?"

Maria was silent.

"Don't be afraid," the artist said then, "I'll get it done in three or four sittings. It will be even better."

In fact he only painted for half an hour when he realized that he was having one of those rare, great days. He painted in silence, without uttering a word.

Maria was silent too. She had been so afraid, so full of unhappy feelings returning to that studio, and now it all seemed so simple, as if there had never been anything between the man who was painting and she who was posing but the admiration and respect of an artist for a model whom he wasn't paying and who had agreed to sit as a favor. If he was so quickly consoled, she thought, if he can look at me as nothing more than someone to paint, it means that he never loved me. Still, just looking at him, you could see he was a man who had suffered terribly. He had always been pale and sickly, but now he seemed moribund, animated by that flash of life that sometimes precedes a deathbed.

"Are you pleased with what you got done today?" she asked him, as she set her hat on her head before leaving.

"Very," said Scipio, rubbing his hands happily together. "I don't think I've ever done anything better."

The following day, a bitter, overcast day that seemed to have plunged them back into winter, Maria's eyes were red again when she arrived. She realized Scipio had noticed.

"I'm sorry," she said, "but you have to work quickly. Not everyone is as good and kind as you are. Coming here is causing me terrible rows."

"Do you want to quit?" Scipio asked quickly, but his voice and gestures betrayed a fear of not being able to complete his work.

"No, does it look like that to you? I want you to finish too. And do it well. Will you exhibit it?"

"I don't think so. And certainly not without your consent."

"Anyway, I beg you, and not out of vanity, believe me, not to make me worse than I am. I know I'm very bad. I've made you suffer a great deal. But it wasn't my fault. It was fate. If you only knew how much I hate myself and how I suffer."

She seemed close to tears, but controlled herself, adding, as she began to pose, "Dear Scipio, do your best work for this painting. I want everyone who knows you to see that a common, silly woman like me, with all her whims, can't harm a man as good as you are."

A week passed, but the portrait, which appeared to please Scipio more every day, this time without the doubts and sudden dampening of enthusiasm that made working a martyrdom for him, wasn't done yet. Maria was still punctual, though it was clear that her punctuality came at a high price for her. Scipio knew it and was grateful to her. A little at a time, perhaps feeling less insecure about himself, he became accustomed to speaking to her as before. He felt that Maria was unhappy, and not only because of the jealous arguments. Or perhaps the arguments were just a pretext that, more than anything else, revealed the worst part of a nature. Something must have happened between the two lovers, something he didn't know about and did nothing to discover, even as he understood how much Maria wanted to take him into her confidence. On the seventh day they seemed to be two old friends; they even spoke about the past. There were some "do you remember?"s uttered by Maria with hidden regrets, and heard by Scipio with smiling sadness.

"It's done," said Scipio one evening, rising, his face transformed. "Look!"

Maria felt her heart constrict, and was trembling as she drew near the canvas. Perhaps it wasn't a masterpiece, but it looked like one to her.

"You're wonderful!" she exclaimed.

Then her eyes suddenly filled with tears, and she leaned her small, graceful head on the artist's shoulder. "Let me, I beg you," she pleaded. "Let me cry."

Scipio let her cry for a long time. He stared at the portrait and barely consoled her with some kind words.

"How great you are and good!" she finally said, drying her eyes and pressing her handkerchief to her mouth as if to stifle her last sobs. "I've always known you to be good and kind. But it's only now that I realize you are the best of men."

Scipio was silent, his head bowed and eyes downcast. Then Maria took one of his hands and covered it with passionate kisses.

"Do you still love me?" she asked him.

Scipio didn't answer. But Maria understood from his silence that he did. That he would love her always, for the rest of his life.

"And I," she said, "love you. Much more now than before."

Scipio shrunk ever more into himself, and stooped as if he had received a fierce blow.

"Do you forgive me?" Maria asked.

"I have nothing to forgive you for," said Scipio softly, so softly that Maria had to bend toward him to hear his words.

"It is myself that I have to forgive, not anyone else. I didn't know how to love you enough." And he looked up at her with those rapturous eyes, in which a flame burned briefly, then flickered out.

"Then," said Maria, "since I love you again, and you still love me. I . . . if you want me to . . . I'll stay." And in her anxiety, she felt her heart skip a beat. "Do you want me to?"

"No," said Scipio softly, "I don't."

The Lottery Numbers

AFTER FOUR YEARS OF MARRIAGE Giuseppe Lara's family life was going along fairly well; that is, there was no evidence of any cracks wrought in it by time. His family wasn't overly large. And he, the head of it, not yet thirty years old, was supporting it as well as he could on a small private income and fees for the reviews and articles he wrote for a large daily newspaper and philosophical journals. He had married young, like all the men of his generation, and could well be considered abstemious. From his manner, which was almost grievously earnest, he appeared to be little inclined to licentiousness in any form. In fact his marriage had been a love match between a man of uncommon talents and hopes and a beautiful woman clever enough to respect her husband's merits and kind enough to bear his many defects and his self-centered personality, at first even with enthusiasm, and later with charitably veiled patience. "Where the sun shines brightest, the shadows are darkest" is the maxim the good woman found underlined in one of Giuseppe's tomes. In terms of her life it meant that a great thinker doesn't also have to be a great family man. Whether she would have preferred to have to forgive her husband for not being philosophical than for not being practical is a question that never entered the young woman's head, so in love was she with Giuseppe and so resolved, as are so many other women, to use all the resources of her feminine nature to make her husband a better man.

She suffered most from their poverty. Giuseppe's income came entirely from an old obligation, which was troublesome to collect, and from his literary earnings, slow to come in and just as troublesome. But this was an issue she didn't like to bring up with her husband. Why hurt him when he himself was trying so hard to improve their lot, even financially? The philosopher's own needs were very limited, and his tastes of an exemplary sobriety. At the table he would say that no delicacy could compare, for those with unspoiled palates, to a simple meal of beans flavored with the purest olive oil. And if during the summer he became thirsty and went into a shop to get a two-penny soda, he would tell the waiter to put in less rather than more syrup. How else to avoid a constant sense of deprivation, except by personally avoiding the need for things? Thus those beans appealed so much to Giuseppe that the only luxury he permitted himself on important occasions was to buy a special kind, which according to him were particularly savory, and whose flavor he never tired of praising, when his wife would have preferred having a chicken thigh, and the children, a box of candy. Lidia wasn't a very vain woman and, though attractive, didn't fuss about her appearance. But the fact is, she would have liked not to have compared so poorly with her friends and old school chums, all of whom had married men who weren't worth her Giuseppe's little finger, and who, when they met her, smiled condescendingly at her inexpensive, worn clothes, or glanced contemptuously at her ears without earrings, her neck without a necklace. Not that it made her angry at her husband; but she couldn't forget the day they went shopping for long-needed necessities (he'd collected a lump sum of three hundred lire that morning for an interminable translation from German), and she'd stopped in front of the window of one of those jewelry shops that cater to women who want to look fashionable but don't have much money, and there, among the other baubles artfully displayed to dazzle passersby, was a pair of coral earrings with their price tag—ten and a half lire. The poor woman had already fallen in love with them, having noticed them when she'd passed the store on her way to the market. And now that her husband had collected so much money, she stopped again to see if they were still there or if some other, luckier woman had already taken them home.

"Look," she said to Giuseppe, indicating the earrings with her eyes as well as with a finger, "do you think those earrings are so bad?"

Giuseppe looked at them distractedly, then said, no, in fact they were pretty and he liked them.

Lidia felt pleased. "Don't you think they look like two drops of blood?" she asked.

"Precisely," Giuseppe agreed, then backed off a few steps to resume his way.

But the woman didn't move. "Ten and a half lire and maybe they'll even let them go for less," she said timidly and without looking at her husband, who, however, could no longer hear her—he was too far away. But she wasn't angry at him. No. Because she was so certain it would never occur to him that there were women in the world who might quiver with desire for a piece of jewelry. Yet with the best will in the world, she could not forget that unavailing stop in front of the pair of earrings.

That difficult and not very happy marriage could have continued on in exactly the same way, for who knows how long, if an unexpected event—a strange conjunction between a dream Lidia had and a lottery drawing—hadn't precipitated a crisis that revealed discord. The young woman dreamed that her dead mother was seated next to her on the edge of her bed and said something like this: "What are you going to do about it, my child? There's no doubt your husband is a wonderful man. God is my witness that I loved him, yet I haven't been very happy since the day you married him. I see that the two of you can't get anywhere this way. You're too poor and the world is too terrible." And at this point she offered her daughter a pinch of tobacco that Lidia, as in the past, accepted just to be polite, pretended to sniff, then secretly threw away. But the old woman, who perceived the pretense, continued with a smile that was both resigned and reproving. "It's not a good idea, my dear girl, to deceive your mother, even about a pinch of tobacco. Why can't you just say right out that you don't want it? But I'm not angry at you. And even though I know your husband doesn't approve of me, I want to give you some advice. Why don't you play the lottery sometimes? You don't risk very much, and what little you do, I can tell you from experience, always comes back, at least in hope. In fact, wait! I'm going to make you a present of three numbers that are definitely coming up this week. Today is Thursday. So you'll still have three days' time to play them." And here it seemed to Lidia that her dear mother bent closer toward her as if she didn't want anyone else to hear, and said slowly into her ear, but so loudly that her voice reverberated within Lidia to the point that it woke her, "Three, sixteen, forty-eight." And all of this occurred with remarkable clarity, as if on a brilliant day, not in a dream. In fact, when Lidia awoke she felt a great tenderness, almost gratitude, and after that, the need to tell Giuseppe every detail while they were having their morning coffee with the children. Giuseppe listened, smiled, then said, "But today isn't Thursday. Just Tuesday. It seems to me that if your mother knows the lottery numbers so well, she should also know the days of the week."

This confused Lidia for a moment, but then she went on, "What's wrong in trying? We can afford the two lire, and just think of all the wonderful things we'd be able to buy with the money if those numbers did come up."

"Stupidity," was Giuseppe's answer.

"Wait a minute. Why is it so stupid? Don't people win on the triple every day, even betting the four numbers? Why can't we at least be lucky in the lottery?"

Giuseppe frowned. "Is that how you feel? That without the lottery we're so unlucky?"

"That's not what I meant. I meant that getting several thousand lire without having to do anything for it would be very nice."

"I explained the whole thing to you a few days ago," Giuseppe said, feeling somewhat irritated. "It's always a losing proposition to bet on the lottery because there's no real correlation between the risk and the earnings. There are other things, roulette, for example, where risk and earnings are almost balanced. I could understand betting on that. But the lottery . . ."

"And my dream?"

"Forget about dreams. You don't believe in them yourself. Fine advice your mother could have given you! If you want me to, I'll be happy to get the probability statistics together and show you again what a snare the lottery is. It's a matter of mathematics."

"I don't know anything about mathematics," said Lidia, looking somewhat pale. "I had a dream. It seems to me that my mother came to me to give me three numbers to bet, and if it were up to me, I'd have played them. But if you don't want to, if you say I'm wrong . . ."

"I certainly don't want to, and certainly you're wrong." And here with the greatest possible clarity and simplicity, Giuseppe reviewed for his wife the probabilities on which the lottery is based. Lidia, who had by then finished her coffee, listened to him intently, her arm around his neck.

"Do you understand?" Giuseppe concluded.

"Completely. And now let's change the subject."

"And even if the numbers do come up, will you still agree that you were better off not playing them?"

Lidia was silent for a moment, then nodded her head.

"Good!" Giuseppe exclaimed. "That's what I like! Now, give me the two lire you wanted to donate to the government and on Sunday I'll bring you a present that costs even more. No, wait. Let's do this. Let's put them in the children's coin bank, and I'll buy you a present anyway."

Lidia smiled and brought over the bank into which two pieces of silver fell while the children clapped their hands. And there was no more talk about it except for a moment at night, in bed, just before they shut the light.

"You still believe," Giuseppe asked, "that we did the right thing to put your two lire in the bank, and not throw them away on the lottery because of a dream?"

"I always believe what you tell me," answered the young woman. And she kissed her husband on the lips.

"Oh, God, how can I be so unlucky?" Lidia said out loud to herself, when she saw her three numbers, 3, 16, and 48, listed in the newspaper among the drawings of the week—and was so upset that she didn't notice where the numbers had come up. "Unlucky me. Unlucky night I listened to my husband!" Beyond her misery at having missed out on the winnings, she felt she had committed a kind of sacrilege in not having followed her dead mother's advice.

"What's the matter, darling? You're so pale?" said Giuseppe, who walked in at that moment carrying a package, evidently the present he had promised his wife. "Where are the children? Did something happen?"

"The three came up."

"What three?"

"My mother's numbers. Three, sixteen, forty-eight."

"Who told you?"

"I saw it in the paper."

Giuseppe was silent for a moment. "And so," he said, "even if they did?"

"Not even if they did. They did."

"I'm not saying they didn't. I'm saying, what's wrong with the fact that those numbers came up instead of others?"

Lidia stared at her husband, irritated and stunned. "What are you talking about?"

"You didn't play them because you understood that the lottery is a bad risk. So why does it bother you now?"

"But if I would have played, I would have won."

Giuseppe shrugged his shoulders. Then he handed Lidia the package he was holding. "It's a shawl," he said. "It cost only a little more than you would have thrown away on the lottery. Tell me if you like it."

Lidia wondered if her husband was crazy and, with trembling hands, undid the package. Inside it was an elegant black silk shawl, clearly chosen with great care. "Thank you," she said, placing the shawl on the table next to the newspaper with not so much as a kiss or a glance for its donor.

"Listen," said Giuseppe, "what's going on? Hadn't we agreed that you wouldn't play? Weren't my reasons correct? And didn't you yourself promise me you'd have no regrets even if the numbers did come up? So what are you crying about?"

Lidia, seated in a corner, was sobbing loudly with her head between her hands.

"Answer me," shouted Giuseppe. "Why are you crying?" And he tried to pull her hands away.

"Now I'm not even allowed to cry."

Giuseppe felt his face turn red. The veins in his head swelled and began pounding.

"Will you please tell me what else I don't allow you to do?" It was the first time the two had argued. In all the four years they'd been married and the two they'd been engaged, they had never gone this far.

"I don't know," said Lidia, "leave me alone."

"With pleasure. But first I want to know what else I don't allow you to do."

Lidia sighed deeply, as if she were about to faint.

"Be careful what you come up with," said Giuseppe. "Tell me, if you can, that I was wrong. And if not . . . if not, you should be ashamed of yourself and stop your crying and complaining. I'd never expect such a thing from you."

"Instead of comforting me, of saying something nice . . ."

"Comfort you for what? For Chri . . . Why can't you just say it right out—tell me what I have to apologize for?"

"What would have been so wrong? It's all your fault I lost so much money."

Giuseppe felt a darkness come before his eyes. In another moment he would even have been capable of murder. And he looked at his wife with more anguish and contempt than any man had ever yet looked at a guilty woman. Then an insult rose to his lips, but he controlled himself and spoke quietly.

"I'm going out to finish my article. When dinner is ready, call me." And he walked toward the door. But then, seeing the newspaper on the table, he couldn't help glancing at it.

"Where are the numbers?" he asked. "I don't see them."

"They're there," said Lidia, drying her eyes, "can't you see them?"

Giuseppe's mouth twisted in an ironical smile. He looked up at his wife and asked, "And where would you have played your numbers?"

"What do you mean, where? I would have played them, that's all. If you hadn't made such a big fuss about it."

"I'm asking you again. Where would you have played those numbers? In Milan, for example, or in Florence, or Bari?"

"What are you talking about, Bari?" Lidia shouted.

"Well, take a look," Giuseppe answered, trying to remain calm. "I see the numbers here, three, sixteen, and forty-eight, but above them I see the word *Bari*. In the other cities, if I am not mistaken, completely different numbers came up. Now I want to know if you really would have bet the money in Bari."

"Let me see," said Lidia.

Giuseppe handed her the paper.

"I would have played them everywhere," she answered, giving it back to him.

Giuseppe broke out laughing. "You're a crazy fool."

"And you're a miserable egotist," Lidia answered, to her misfortune. "You got three hundred lire all at once and you refused to buy me a pair of earrings for ten and a half."

"What earrings? What are you talking about?" asked Giuseppe, looking at her so fiercely that the young woman could hardly stand his eyes on her and began shivering with fear. But it was just that, that made her demon urge her on.

"And you never brought home any candy for those poor children. They have thick blood from eating your beans."

"For Chri . . . ," Giuseppe shouted again, and tore his hands through his hair. His forehead was burning, and he knew that if he didn't get out immediately, he would strike that monstrous woman. He walked around the room twice, then went to the door.

"When my beans are done," he said, "call me, so I can eat."

And he walked out of that hellish place, where it had taken less than a quarter of an hour to effect a family's misfortune, and dissolve a long and true love. Because, if after that terrible scene, the philosopher didn't separate from his wife, it was only because life rarely concedes such neat solutions to the poor. And notwithstanding an apparent reconciliation a few days later, he began feeling more and more alone and alienated, and spent entire days in his tiny study thinking about his unhappiness and about the evil that would befall the world if women, with their irremediable irrationality, had power.

The Hen

ODONE GUASTI, who, later in life and under another name, would acquire a modicum of fame in the republic of letters, became an apprentice in the office and warehouse of a small firm dealing in citrus fruits in Trieste before his fifteenth birthday. The boy had given up classical studies, for which he felt ill-suited, for a business career in a rapture of happiness. Hadn't he thought that perhaps he'd been born for business? But in little less than a month of sorting crates of oranges and writing in registry books, he'd been overtaken by the same fundamental restlessness he'd felt in the face of his scribbled-in and scrawled-over, ministry-approved Greek and Latin texts. He hated his employer, who exploited his clear handwriting and long adolescent legs, almost as much as he had hated the head of his form, and despised an old employee, the only person he worked with, just as he'd despised classmates who had been adept at getting high grades and staying in the good graces of their superiors. Unwarranted hatreds, of course, but it would take many years and much suffering before Odone, rethinking his past and comparing it to his present, would understand that he had been completely in the wrong, and that he would never have made a good scholar or a good employee. It is an invaluable privilege of maturity to rediscover that the roots of one's problems are in oneself. Young people can only blame the outside world and rage against it in proportion to their defects. But who, for that matter, could have explained Odone to himself, could have corrected him to any effect, when even before his birth his father had disappeared, never to return, and when he lived alone with his mother, a disconsolate and impoverished woman whose sole desire in life was that her only child be healthy and earn enough soon enough to extricate them both from a humiliating dependence on relatives? Rachele Guasti loved her son with an almost sinful intensity, with that embittered maternal love peculiar to women whose marriages end in disaster. And he, the boy, the object of that love, had until then returned it in kind, though his was shaded with egotism, because parents love for what they give, and children for what they receive. There is a moment in the life of a child, just before filial love dies in reaction to family life, and to love itself, when it emits its last and most brilliant flame. And so, those rare souls who enjoyed walking the semideserted Sant'Andrea promenade could, on holiday afternoons, see Odone strolling arm in arm with his mother, he already in long pants with the hint of a mustache on his upper lip, she, much shorter, wearing a black veil and a piteously small, strange hat on her head. So, too, after dinner, mother and son would have sweet and quiet talks together, in which the differences between them, though becoming apparent to the boy, were not yet such, because he still believed in their common future, as to cause him to revolt or destroy their idyll by quarreling. To his mother Odone was still a child, who before going to bed at night remembered to thank God for having given him the most beautiful, the best, and the wisest of all the mothers living for the sake of their children's happiness, in His wonderful, never sufficiently praised, work of Creation.

And so it was that Odone was thinking of how happy his mother would be to hear about the heartfelt and appreciative "thank you" he'd uttered to his boss one evening at the end of the month, when the latter had tossed a bank note on his table announcing, "From today on, you'll be paid. Ten crowns a month." It was the first money he'd ever earned. How surprised that dear, ill-rewarded woman would be when he put the money in her hand and said, "Take it, Mamma, it's for you," which they would both understand as, "And it's nothing compared to what I'll do for you some-day."

With those ten crowns, any doubts about a business career that would have had time to develop in Odone in another few months of apprenticeship disappeared. And with them went the qualms of regret he always felt when out on some errand he would meet an ex-schoolmate and try—alas, in vain—to convince him how much better off he, Odone, was to have left school for work, only to suffer insults or silences that implied, "Sure, but let's see what happens in a couple of years, flunky."

At the end of the day he raced home and, heart pounding like that of a lover bringing a first gift to his sweetheart, dashed up the stairs; then stammering and kissing his mother, he gave her the great news. Signora Rachele was thrilled (though less so than Odone had hoped) and forgave the boy for having upset her when he'd refused to eat his soup at lunch, the memory of which had made the pleasure he expected to give her when he returned home even more precious to him. In the end she wanted Odone to use half the money for himself, for his own pleasure. However, she cautioned him to spend it as conscientiously as he had earned it, and reminded him of certain dangers about which boys are more often warned by fathers than mothers. For to Rachele Guasti, who never uttered certain

words or even implied them by circumlocution without first spitting on
the ground (so great was the disgust they caused her), had fallen the
unpleasant task of explaining them to her son. And in her dire need she
did so to the best of her ability, so that she might please God and sleep
in peace with a clear conscience.

Needless warnings. Odone wasn't yet interested in women, and never
walked through those alleys crowded evenings with sailors and loud-
voiced women without hurrying his steps. Besides, he had already decided
how to spend his five crowns: on a present for his mother. His only
problem was choosing between a round snuff box decorated with silver
and a black fan with sequins. But since man proposes and God disposes,
no one, no matter how strong his generous intentions, can feel himself
safe from temptation. And if temptation didn't overcome Odone in the
guise of a human female, it did in that of a beautiful hen. And now I will
tell you how and why he couldn't resist her, and about the bitter price he
paid.

The following day around two in the afternoon Odone, who had left
home to return to work determined not to enter his prison a moment sooner
than necessary, and who was dawdling in Trieste's Ponte Rosso square,
where there was and still is a market for live birds and poultry, stopped
to look at the caged wares. At first he was struck by exotic, flame-bright
birds that seemed live incarnations of the postage stamps issued by some
British colonies and primitive statelets that he'd often admired in his
modest collection. Then his heart went out to a blackbird, a completely
mysterious looking creature in whose beak a half-dozen tiny worms wrig-
gled, which the bird swallowed one at a time, each time demonstrating
its pleasure by half-closing its round eyes circled with the same fine gold
as its beak. He took little pleasure in the parrots and was revolted by a
monkey. In the end, he was attracted to the chickens jammed into narrow
wooden cages from which their necks projected while they complained
acrimoniously or blamed each other for their thirst and lack of space. It
wasn't gluttony that had stirred Odone's emotions. He loved live chickens
and was unhappy to see them served at the table. On his long, solitary
walks in the countryside, the kind of walks that in adolescence can be as
long as a forced march and as solemn as a conquest, when he saw some
in front of a farmhouse or through a vista of green fields, ridges, and
wattles, he would rejoice in the sight as if it were a painting in which his

emotions of the moment were concentrated. And he would reach out happily to stroke a hen so domesticated or perhaps so overcome by flight-impeding terror that she couldn't escape his loving gesture. Whereas others heard unpleasant and monotonous sounds emanating from a henhouse, Odone heard ever-changing music, particularly toward evening when the half-asleep hens lamented in their softest voices.

He found the rooster less appealing. The pride and magnanimity that farmyard sultan demonstrates when he uncovers a grub or other tasty morsel, and struggles visibly to overcome his own great greed before finally leaving it to a female, cannot be appreciated except by a mature man, someone capable of understanding the magnificent power of renunciation and the masculine gallantry inherent in every true sacrifice. If, during those years, anyone had asked Odone why he was so fond of the stupid birds that everyone else associated only with food, he couldn't have answered. In fact, many people did ask him and it took him twenty years to reply. And when he did, it was with a poem, and that, too, was barely understood. To him, those tiny feathered bodies were imbued with the essence of airiness, of the countryside, and of the changing hours of the day. But in addition to these aesthetic reasons, there was another, sentimental one. Brought up without brothers, sisters, or friends, Odone had spent a great deal of time during his childhood playing with a hen. His mother had bought it intending to kill it for food, but such and so many had been the boy's pleas that she had finally agreed to let it live and roam the house as if it were a dog. From that day on, not only could the boy drink still warm eggs, but he had a companion. Even his mother eventually enjoyed the hen's panicky leaps against the doors and windows of the kitchen, to which it retreated on the rare occasions when they had company. And when, sweaty and breathless, basket in hand, Signora Rachele returned from marketing to see Cò-cò (as she and the boy had decided to name the bird) come running toward her, beak open, wings outspread and aflutter, she would say admiringly, "And they say hens are stupid." But often, too, it would gall the mother to see her son talking to a chicken as if it were a person. It seemed to her almost a sign of idiocy. To Odone, however, the hours he spent with the hen were truly his own; whether he had her sit, perch, really, next to him on the brick steps between the kitchen and the dining room, steps that turned a strange red in the setting sun and reminded him of the steps outside purgatory that he'd seen in a religious painting, or whether, hugging her so tightly to him that she shrieked, and happy in his belief that he had so much time ahead to live and enjoy the pleasures of the world (and thereafter, he'd have all eternity), he would talk to Cò-cò about daring deeds and journeys, and about future joys, in effect, about everything that went through his head. But after two years of domestic restrictions and of overly appetizing, cooked foods, the heart of that strange, enraptured victim of childhood burst (as a neighbor who heard about it said), burst because she had become too fat. (She'd looked like an odalisk.) In short, she died and was buried by her friend. Odone wanted another hen instantly, a request his mother categorically refused. He was too old for that now. His stamp album and taking walks with her were, had to be, recreation enough for him.

However, an unsatisfied desire is a lasting desire. And Odone, standing in front of caged chickens with his first earnings in his pocket, felt its stirrings. One chicken in particular appealed to him. She was beautiful, with a small, expressive head, brilliant black plumage, and a long arched tail that reminded Odone of the feathers in Bersaglieris' hats. He asked the price more out of curiosity than any intention to buy it (thinking it would cost a fortune). And the vendor, surprised by a customer whose age and sex were so unusual, answered curtly, as if he were wasting his breath, "Three crowns and a half."

"So little," Odone said.

The man stared at him more irked than astonished, and more certain than ever that he was the butt of some joke. But as he came to realize that the boy was serious, he opened the cage and removed the bird, fluffing her feathers so his customer could see her plumpness and the appealing color of her flesh.

"That's enough," said Odone, upset by the bird's shrill cries and the efforts she was making to hold her head up so as not to choke. "I'll take her," he went on, "but you have to send her to my house immediately."

"Immediately," repeated the little man and, calling over an errand boy, handed him the chicken by the legs. Odone paid, gave the boy his address, plus twenty cents as a tip, and told him to give his (Odone's) name to the person who answered the door. Then he looked at the clock. It was almost a quarter past two, and rushing off to his office, he began trying to convince himself that he had spent his money wisely. He did it by exaggerating the joy he would feel to find Cò-cò alive when he returned home. But the more he struggled to escape them, the more he was struck by thoughts, suspicions that he had done something useless, even foolish. He thought that Cò-cò was dead once and for all and all the chickens in the world could never replace her; that his childhood had died too and that it was crazy to want to recreate its tenderness outside of memory; that his mother's hair was already completely white, that she was tiring ever more quickly, and that she might die before he could fulfill his promise to ease her life; that he had been wrong to leave school for a job; and that a mistake had been made in his life, what it was or how it happened he didn't know, but it was a mistake, a sin that weighed more heavily on his heart every day, one, the boy thought, that had befallen only him, not yet knowing (as he would only too well, later) that his pain was the pain of all mankind, of every human life: the pain religion calls Original Sin.

Outside the warehouse, laborers were waiting for Odone with a load of orange crates and he soon lost himself in the work of marking and sorting. Then he wrote out invoices, transcribed the draft of a long letter his boss had left in his best business hand, went out to do an errand at the other end of town, came back with a reply, went out again to pay for cargo insurance at the Adria shipping association, sealed the letters, wrote addresses on their envelopes, stamped them, and finally, helped the porter lock up. He would normally also have had to rush down to the post office to be sure the letters went out that day, but this particular evening, as soon as he was out of the owner's sight, he threw them into the first mailbox he saw and went home almost at a run. His mother, who had been waiting for him at a window, opened the door without asking who was there. She took his hat from him and handed him the jacket he wore at home. Then she spoke.

"Thank you," she smiled at him. "Thank you for that beautiful present. How much did you pay for it?"

"Three crowns, fifty," Odone answered cheerfully. "Plus twenty cents for a tip. That's not much, is it?" He was happily surprised that his mother had so cheerfully accepted the interdicted animal that soiled wherever it went and really belonged outdoors, not in a house, as a gift for herself.

"Where is she?" he said. "I want to see her."

The housewife opened a door. There behind it, hanging from a nail, the hen, plucked clean and stiff in death, froze Odone's heart.

"I don't know how you managed to find such a nice plump one," said his mother. "It's almost more a capon than a hen. You really have an eye for it. Tomorrow, I'll get a piece of beef and make you a wonderful soup. Tonight, though, you'll have to settle for vegetables. The poor creature was so full of eggs, it was almost a sin to have killed her."

Odone couldn't bear to listen to another word and fled to his room. His heart was beating furiously and tears burned in his eyes, tears not only for the chicken's miserable death, a fate so different from the one he'd planned, but because his mother, his own mother, had not understood him. Was such a thing possible? That a mother not understand her son? That to be understood by his mother, a boy had to explain himself as if to a total stranger? Is that the way all mothers were (ten years later he would say women) or only his own? He had little desire to talk, yet when the guilty woman entered his room carrying a lit oil lamp, Odone resolved to tell her about the misunderstanding, about the enormous pain that she, though unintentionally, had caused him.

Signora Rachele shrugged her shoulders, was surprised, became angry, and said that a boy who was going to be fifteen years old in two months doesn't play with hens anymore. Then she asked if he'd like to go out for a while, because supper wasn't ready yet, and a short walk would do him good.

"Who killed her?" Odone asked.

"I did. Why do you ask?"

"Because I thought you didn't have the heart to kill chickens."

"When I was a girl, I couldn't have done it," Signora Rachele answered, "not even for a hundred crowns. But ever since I've been a mother it doesn't bother me in the least. When you were recovering from typhus, I would wring a cock's neck with pleasure, thinking of the wonderful broth it would make for you."

Odone, still confused, didn't answer, because he had the feeling that he had more to say to himself on the subject than to anyone else. But from that evening on, he loved his mother less and less.

The Interpretation

WALKING ONE DAY on the Via Barriera Vecchia in Trieste, Lina suddenly put her hand on my arm and said to me, "Look! Look at that woman across the street going in the opposite direction from us, the one holding the roll of music and running as if someone's chasing her. Do you see her? Hurry, take a good look. But don't let her see you."

I looked. And saw a small woman of undetermined age, dressed a little like an unflirtatious working girl and a little like an impoverished widow, with a tiny hat on her head, the kind old ladies wear, all spangles and veil. She had a slight limp and was hurrying down the street as if someone were breathlessly awaiting her. Altogether she looked so strange that if my dog had seen her, there's no doubt he would have barked at her. I saw that she was holding something rolled up in her hand, but I couldn't be sure it was music.

"Well?" I said, "so what?"

Lina smiled faintly. It was one of those smiles that seem to be hiding tears, the kind people with morbid sensitivities generally smile. I call them "heartsick smiles." There's no doubt that whatever causes them is either dreadful or mildly ridiculous.

"That woman is studying singing. And right now" (it was one in the afternoon) "she's rushing to a lesson."

"But she's an old lady," I exclaimed.

"Not quite. She's thirty-five[1] or a little over."

"And she's studying singing? Why? Does she enjoy it that much?"

"What do you mean enjoy? She's doing it to become a prima donna. She's been studying for ten years. You should only know the story!"

"Is she at least rich?"

"Rich! She's a seamstress. She works ten to twelve hours a day for one of those women who sell the linen they stitch up in the Via Nuova, you know the kind—may God curse them!—who work their employees into consumption and buy themselves three-story houses. Ten years ago, one of those women, her boss, happened to hear her sing some song or other to herself and told her, 'Adelina Patti was a poor girl, a working girl like you, but right off she found someone to give her lessons for

---

[1] *Saba's note:* The equivalent of fifty years, these days.

nothing and even to pay her expenses. Then when she became *the* Patti, she rewarded her teacher and the person who had first praised her singing.'"

"Why did she tell her that? To tease her?"

"Maybe not. It's possible at the moment she really liked her voice. But the fact is that from that time on, the poor thing never again had a minute of peace. She immediately went looking for a teacher. She started asking the most famous in town, but they were expensive—charged too much for what she was earning. So she went looking for someone smart, someone who, on hearing her first note, would realize what a treasure she had in her throat. And she found someone, my dear. She found someone."

"Really?"

"Yes, indeed, darling. And sooner than you'd think. Not a man, but a woman, an old lady of seventy who taught the old techniques, the good ones singers long ago used, you know, the kind of singers we used to hear when we were young, who aren't around anymore even at La Scala. She studied continuously, four or five years with the same old lady, then one evening . . . But no, I can't. I really can't. My Lord!" And here Lina stopped to laugh even more sadly, with one hand on her chest. It really seemed she wouldn't be able to go on.

"And then?" I asked, though I began to feel a kind of anxiety and shame.

"Then, one evening, four or five years ago, she gave a concert at the Liceo. A concert, you know, in public, but at her teacher's expense. I was there," she said, almost whispering.

"You were there?" I shuddered.

"No, I can't. I can't tell you. It hurts me too much. A dress, you know, white, the whole outfit, something she made at home. Too tight, too short, thrown together out of necessity. The kind of thing that breaks your heart. And then you had to see the way she came in, walked up to the podium, bowed."

"But how was her singing?"

"Can't you imagine? Everything—voice, training, program—it all went with those clothes. But I couldn't take it. After two or three pieces, I left."

"And the audience? Did they applaud?"

"The audience applauded after every piece. Two or three short claps, then there'd be silence. Icy silence, like in a waiting room."

"And did she understand?"

"And how she understood! She knew it wasn't the great success she hoped it would be. But she blamed everything on her teacher. The friend who took me to the concert and told me the whole story was there when she and the teacher had it out. The girl accused the teacher of having ruined her. The teacher accused the girl of ingratitude and being nasty. Finally they both began to cry like a pair of little girls and embraced each other. The old woman admitted it was her fault, that she was no longer good for anything. She asked the girl's forgiveness for the five years she'd caused her to lose, and then she suggested that she find another, younger teacher, someone who used more acceptable modern techniques. She offered to help her with expenses. The girl was thirty-one at the time."

"And she's still studying?"

"Let me finish. The old woman really helped her with expenses, but just a little, as much as she could afford. So, to pay her new teacher, who must certainly have charged more, she not only had to put in her twelve hours at the shop, but she also would take things home that she worked on at night. She studied at lunchtime and a little in the evening as soon as she got home. The teacher kept giving her lessons for another two years, listening to her dreams and encouraging them, agreeing with her that the fault lay with this thing or that thing, which had nothing to do with her. Then, one day, even he became tired of that comedy and told her straight out that he didn't think she'd ever be a prima donna, but that with time she might become good enough for second leads. In the meantime, if she were willing to try it out and earn some money, he advised her to join the chorus of a second-string opera company, at least for a while. He himself would send a letter of recommendation to the chorus master, who was a friend of his."

"And the prima donna?"

"Agreed to it. Why, I don't know. But she did. She stopped going to the shop and scraped along on the work she did at home and on what she earned at the chorus. But you know what? The other women in the chorus were there to get their three or four crowns an evening. If anything, they were thrilled to be in the chorus and to be singing at the opera house. But she . . . with her air of being an unappreciated prima donna, her obsession with getting this or that famous soprano to listen to her, being less talented and less well prepared than the others . . . she ended up being thoroughly disliked by everyone. And she was let go. Or she quit."

"Poor thing."

"And she went on studying. But with another teacher, because the previous one didn't want her back. He told her that she was too much of a nuisance, that the only reason she'd been in the chorus was because of him. A fine thing she'd done for his reputation! And besides, it seems he was a boor. At least she told my friend that all men are boors like her singing teacher. That's why she had decided never to marry—that she would die a spinster."

"And now?"

"Now, I don't know with whom, but I'm sure she's still studying, and still has great hopes. Didn't you see the way she was running? Do you think there could possibly be a more unhappy woman than she? Or a more heartbreaking situation than hers?"

"No," I answered, "I don't." And then we dropped the subject.

But I brought it up again, after several years and a full life. One evening, after dinner, I asked Lina if she still remembered that linen seamstress and future prima donna whose story she'd told me so many years ago in the Via Barriera Vecchia in Trieste. "At that time," I said to her, "I agreed with you when you wondered if there could be a sadder case in the whole world. Now, with all my long experience of living, it seems to me we were wrong. Actually, I want to give you a different interpretation of the facts."

"Different in what way?"

"Different in the sense that though I don't think we can call her a fortunate woman, perhaps she wasn't really that, but neither was she more unhappy than many women, than those who were successful, Adelina Patti, for example, or than those who have husbands or lovers who adore them."

"I don't follow you."

"Because you're thinking only of the impression that her life made on you but not how it felt to her, who was living it. You're seeing things from the point of view of an observer, not from that of the patient. But think for a minute what her life would have been like without that heaven-sent blunder that filled her heart with so much hope and gave a poor, homely woman a passion for something the rest of the world didn't believe in. Now she's almost a martyr, instead of being just any old spinster because she was unattractive, had no money, or didn't use any of the wiles that even poor and crippled women use to get husbands.

"What could her life have been like before that woman at the shop gave her hope that she might become as rich and famous as Adelina Patti? She herself must have seen it clearly—a life bounded entirely by that shop on the Via Nuova and by her small furnished room, and ending with a pauper's funeral, attended—maybe—by one or two old ladies like herself. But it was altogether different from the moment she began to study singing, from the day that teacher (the old lady with the good techniques) told her she would give her lessons free because her voice and talent warranted it. Her heart must have been pounding; she must have been as overcome with emotion as other young girls are at their first kiss. It opened a window into her soul through which the infinite could enter, or at least as much of the infinite as can enter such a young woman's soul. Imagine her happiness at her early progress (or presumed progress—it doesn't make any difference), or at her first aria, the day she first sang an aria from some well-known, classic work, something she might have heard her mother sing or hum over and over again, maybe from *The Huguenots* or *The Prophet?*

"Certainly she must have suffered a great deal at the shop—felt herself locked in a prison full of shop boys and girls, all younger than she, all outdoing each other in teasing her, none of whom (out of jealousy) took her ambition seriously. But for her, what pleasures, what problems, what an orgy of plans and projects, what secret places in her soul of which the others knew nothing and where she alone could find refuge during the long working day. And how much she must have longed for Sundays, when she could spend the entire day studying and practicing her favorite pieces! How would she have spent her Sunday afternoons, otherwise? Playing lotto in a neighbor's room? And when she went to the opera (and she certainly must have gone and as often as possible—what better way was there to learn?) and heard the applause and saw the flowers thrown at the woman who stood where she would stand one day, whether in a year or two it hardly mattered. What's even ten years of waiting compared to the joy of such a triumph? And no one, no one except for herself and that old teacher, believed in her. They even ridiculed her. The jealous idiots! But the more she felt she was being ridiculed, the more fervent her passion became. The truth is that she was living, when otherwise she would have merely vegetated. How many times, bent over her sewing machine, recalling some private thought, must she have felt her heart leap (so to speak) into her throat and a desire to release her overflowing soul in beautiful song, to startle and astonish her coworkers, except that their ears were always closed by ignorance and by envy of her, whom they tormented. Compared with all that, how important could the fiasco of the concert be, or the humiliation in the chorus, or the many years already gone by in which no impresario had come to her door (he really should have passed beneath her window and heard her singing, accidentally, it had to be accidentally) with a top hat and signed contract in hand? I despair for such blunders in the strong, but in the weak, in the very weakest, no. In fact they make me believe in a Divine Providence that feeds small, homeless creatures and offers illusions of artistry to those poor hysterical souls who are too inept for ordinary life. Because there's no doubt your friend's friend is a hysteric, one of those women who as nuns can achieve sainthood; or at least she's an ordinary hysteric. Don't you see that her whole life revolved around one idea? She believed in what her employer told her, as others believe in their dreams or hallucinations."

"But after that day the woman did nothing but laugh at her. Our budding prima donna is the least of what the girl had to tolerate from her."

"It doesn't mean anything. That thirty-five-year-old shop girl with her unhappy passion lived more intensely than the other woman with her three-story house."

"But will she ever understand? And what then?"

"Later, very much later. Later than you can even imagine. And possibly, also, never. It would be too terrible for a human being whose life has been a failure to have to face the fact that the failure itself and the defect that caused it came from within her and from nowhere else. Instead, she's certain to continue believing what she does now and, at some point in the future, to be even more firmly convinced of it. Her employer's prophecy, the teacher's free lessons, the concert at the Liceo and the public's applause (whether due to convention or compassion), the ironic or pitying encouragement of the well-known women whom she persuaded to hear her sing, a flattering success performing at a friend's house—these and other occasions we know nothing about will in time take on in her fantasies the proportion and meaning of the triumphs she aspired to. Adelina Patti may not have more memories or better ones than this poor old woman, whose eyes soon won't be good enough for sewing and those indigence will enable her employer to profit still more by paying her less and less. Believe me, my dear, that's the way it is."

"I like your interpretation," Lina said. "But I don't think it's right."

War Dream

I DREAMED I WAS IN A WAR—but not in one of the many recent ones. No, I was a lone outpost in the army of King Charles Albert in the territory between Lombardy and Piedmont on a sultry morning in 1848 or '49.

The battles for independence (our name for them) or the Italian campaign (the enemy's name) are closer to our hearts even now than the conquest of Tripoli or the upheavals in the Balkans. Perhaps our fathers lived them so intensely that they transmitted a detailed sense of place—almost a visual impression—to their descendants, just as they transmitted hair color or a particular gait. There's no doubt that the site at which I found myself in the dream must have existed and still exists somewhere in those regions. And it's not impossible that I might one day see it and even recognize it.

Have you ever felt, particularly toward dawn, just before a window is opened or an intruding voice wakes you abruptly, that you dreamed about something from your past, perhaps a school memory, completely unimportant in itself, and which when it occurred couldn't have given you either pleasure or pain but that, nevertheless, reexperienced in a dream is accompanied by a new sense of happiness, a feeling of paradise troubled only by the fear that the enchantment would end? I felt something like that when I dreamed I was lying on the grass in the shelter of a thicket, my rifle at the ready to fire my first shot in the service of my country and of good King Charles Albert on that sultry morning in 1848 or '49.

How long would I have been in that prescribed immobile position? I don't know. I only know that after a few minutes or a few hours, a feeling, not really fear, but a vague apprehension deep in my heart, disappeared completely. I no longer thought of myself as a living target, and forgetting both danger and the possibility of punishment, I turned around to lie on my back with my eyes toward heaven, feeling as blissful as a boy spending his day, morning to evening, afloat on his back in the sea, with time out only for lunch on the beach. I had been thinking that the campaign, which had begun so well—with several victories—would start going badly for us and that the future would be worse than the past. But even this foreboding of Novara so painful to the heart of an ardent patriot, which I certainly was in those days, was overcome by the stillness and languor of the countryside illuminated by the near-midday sun. Crickets were chirping. The corn was ripe and high. There was no sound of gunfire near or far and the smoke that rose from the cottages of the ancient little village wasn't incendiary. A few yoked black-and-white cows were grazing on the summit of a hill where the clouds had moved off to reveal blueness like the eye of God. So the lone sentinel felt happy and at peace, as only those sitting at a window in their homes after a good day's work have a right to feel, or those who, during a war, find themselves in it dreaming and knowing they are dreaming.

Not a Croat in sight and no hate for the enemy. I began thinking about old Radetsky with his wrinkled face under the green feathered hat of a field marshal—so old that he could no longer mount a horse. I could see him in his study intent on planning a retreat or an attack, leaning against a table or perhaps the back of a chair so as not to fall. I thought of him without any hostility, something quite natural today but iniquitous in 1849. And I entertained myself imagining the scene when the armistice broke down and he entered the campaign—how with all the noise coming from the crowds under the commander's window, his troops had persuaded him to add the verdant leaf, badge of the Austrian soldier, to the buttonhole of his heavily decorated jacket. Certainly his rabble troops, conscripts or veterans, must all have loved him. How could they not love an eighty-six-year-old who was still winning battles and defending two provinces for his emperor? Haven't we all been fond of some old person already so old when we were children that it seemed impossible that he could still be living? Even knowing that the person can't go on much longer, the thought of his approaching and inevitable death becomes more terrifying than the premature death of a youth. Why should Radetsky—who had fought so many campaigns against Napoleon, who knew Frederick the Great and other eminent men of an era so much more vivid than the present, and of which he was one of the last witnesses—have to die? He had lived so long that . . . Those, more or less, must have been the feelings the enemy had for their old and glorious marshal, though perhaps they were not as aware of them as I've made out here.

Anyway, instead of being on guard, I was spending my time thinking about my enemies' feelings. And the thought and image of Radetsky merged strangely on that languorous afternoon with my love for a very old aunt of mine and the din of distant armies, when suddenly the sound of footsteps somewhere down the road called me again to the state of mind of a sentry and I turned my head toward the sound. The road passed between two hills. I was posted on one of them about a hundred feet from another guard. On the opposite hill, which I was supposed to be watching for any change—to be signaled with a rifle shot—everything was still except for slight movements of the foliage and the cows at the summit. Now, finally, here was the enemy. Or rather just one—an Austrian, bent under the weight of his knapsack and of his characteristically stiff and conical cap, with his gun trailing behind him. He was walking unconcernedly down the road controlled by my rifle, as sure of himself and of his life as if it were a time of peace—as if on completing a long drill he had stayed behind a little to satisfy some need and was now leisurely rejoining his outfit.

When I had already raised the barrel of my gun and my index finger was on the trigger, a happy thought crossed my mind, or rather, a cheerful consciousness of the absolutely irreversible act I was about to commit, a thought that delayed the act for a few seconds. Because my regiment had just been stationed at the front and my company had only that morning been given the honor of providing guards for these advanced positions, this would be the first (and, I was hoping, not the last) shot that I would fire against a living target, not only in the few months since the war began but in my entire life. And that soldier walking unwarily down that lonely road would be the first person to die by an act of my will and by virtue of my firearm. I wanted, as I said, to fully feel this new sensation. Meanwhile the Austrian had continued walking, and the closer he got to me, the larger and clearer he became in the sights of the rifle pointed at his chest. I knew that though I wasn't great at marching, I was a very good shot. At that short distance, and without any awareness of his predicament, how could he possibly escape me?

No, he certainly wouldn't get away. So I had plenty of time to think about myself and contemplate my every sensation without fear that in doing so I would fail my first test as a soldier. In fact, that very morning before sending us out to these positions, our captain had warned us one last time not to fire unless we were certain that each shot would result in a kill. Thus we wouldn't waste ammunition or give away our position for no good reason. It was therefore to obey my captain that I had not yet fired. And then, too, I wanted to see my victim's face. He seemed to be a Croat (Austrian troops in 1848 were all Croats), and that reminded me of the attacks and the violence Italians had suffered at the hands of these barbarians, so that I would have struck him the fearful blow with the deepest and warmest pleasure, not merely as at some vague enemy.

For now the soldier was continuing on with absolutely no sense of the danger he was in. He didn't look toward the right or the left. He wasn't trying to hide, nor was he taking longer steps as you do passing a lonely spot at night when you feel the darkness pressing upon your back. And that poor boy had so much darkness at his back. His few moments in the sweet sunlight were completely in my hands. Only I could decide whether he was to have one more or one less. All that was required was the precise movement of my index finger for him to be overtaken by a sudden fear, a sudden spasm, then feel himself falling for all eternity onto that road in a foreign country without seeing who had harmed him, and with no other witnesses but the two of us, to my shot and his fall, except that silent countryside under that clouded sky. And the people who would eventually learn about it could do nothing but praise me. Though perhaps not even that—because one neither blames nor praises a hungry person who, on finding a laden table, eats—nor someone who (during a war, of course) kills an enemy who happens into his gun sights.

It was simple and easy, so simple and so easy that he had already walked about fifty paces and I—posted there for that specific purpose and having walked so many kilometers and gone through so much turmoil to get there—had not yet struck. Now he was almost upon me. Sweat was running from under his silly kepi along his beardless, sunburned face, a trivial face, neither attractive nor unattractive, but most importantly without the characteristics of his kind that I was expecting would give me that last spur to shoot him. In fact, he looked so insignificant that I thought to myself, "This is the enemy?" And I can still remember that I felt strangely disappointed and annoyed.

Obviously the boy was returning from some mission for his regiment as he would have done in normal times and in friendly territory. Or perhaps he was an orderly for some big shot who, like a tradesman with his own shop boy, had sent him on an errand to a friend. Then either the boy had gotten lost on his way back or the officer who'd sent him out didn't know there were advance troops so close by. He was carrying a package under his left arm (it looked like laundry wrapped in a red military handkerchief) and trailing his gun in the other to relieve his shoulder of the numbing weight. The only thing I couldn't understand was why he was also carrying his knapsack. Why hadn't he left it in his tent? On the whole he had a very peaceful appearance, hardly a warrior or an enemy. I'd seen such types on our side too, among the orderlies and soldiers assigned to barracks duty. But even with that perfectly imbecilic face, who knows how many Italians he had already killed—and how many more he would still kill, given the opportunity. By God, no! He was just across from me now, almost skimming the thicket through which I was aiming my rifle. I could already hear the small sound his knapsack was making against his back and his deep, heavy breathing, the breathing of a thirsty dog on a hot August day. A short moment of dizziness, a moment in which all is red, and then in that sudden rain of blood, a shameful and paralyzing thought. And his mother?

Precisely. So though it was a shameful thing for a soldier facing the enemy, now that I've returned to my bookish life, I have to confess that I, an Italian soldier in 1848 or '49, put off killing an Austrian solely by force of the thought that the boy no doubt had a mother. Perhaps the thought wouldn't have occurred to me if the soldier had been a man of my kind—an artist, a writer, a man of greater spirituality. But since it was a matter of his being half a beast—how could I not think of him as a peasant—a Croatian woodsman, whom his parents probably considered a genuine treasure? Who knows how much his mother had suffered, after bringing him up, to have to hand him over on the appointed day to the emperor and Field Marshal Radetsky? Why hadn't the thought of his coming pain occurred to me before—the heartrending cry of an animal receiving its death blow (I was certain that he would cry out), the fall after a short attempt to keep standing, with his kepi already on the ground and his head between his hands (I had never yet seen soldiers fall except in regimental prints), the brief death struggle in the dust, and so on and so forth—as had the distant sufferings of his family and the certainty that for this moment at least it was up to me and to me alone whether his mother would get the news from the village priest, "Your son is dead," or whether she would see the boy come back from war alive and well. As for the boy himself, I was sure it would be a good thing to shoot him. It would rid us of a marksman, remove him from the effort, the dangers and terrors of armed warfare, and from that other much longer and strenuous war against poverty and vice that he would have to battle all the rest of his life. But his mother, his family, the people who were waiting . . .

And by then he had passed me. I could no longer kill him with a shot in the chest. I'd have to shoot him in the back.

In the back! Like a deserter. Like a traitor. When in truth he was neither, just lost. And I would have fired my rifle for the first time against an essentially unarmed enemy. Wouldn't it have been less than noble, less than generous, less than military, and (remember that this is 1848) less than Italian? And there was something else in me too. Something heavy and burdensome, but which worked to the advantage of the enemy, who had by now reached a turning. Another few steps and it would have been almost as difficult for me to kill him as it would have been for his family to revive him if I had done what it was my duty to have done at the right time, and for which that morning I had been sent to that particular place and no other on the face of the earth. Because by now, even if I wanted to do it, it was too late. And that heavy and burdensome feeling, like the pangs of remorse or anger one feels when one has stupidly let the opportunity to do a good deed go by, was now confounded with a strange and inexplicable growing terror of raising my eyes to the opposite hill. I was so afraid to do it that I finally had to, to keep my chest from bursting. I raised my head and looked around. Ten, a hundred, a thousand, a hundred thousand soldiers, all of Austria was sliding slowly down from the summit of that hill. Every rifle in good Field Marshal Radetsky's army was pointed at my head. And those faces! Howling faces, sweaty and filthy with blood and dust, twisted in scorn. Because every single one of them knew what I had, or more correctly, what I had not done. In addition to the enemy's bullets, I had earned its derision. Quite a job I'd done of protecting the hill entrusted to my watch! But the little soldier was alive and his mother would clasp him to her when he came back home!

A sudden deafening and terrible roar shook me from the dream that had become an incubus and brought me back to the reality of everyday life. But the dream had been so like at least a part of that reality, that though it wouldn't be right, it still wouldn't be wrong to say that I had dreamed with my eyes open.

How I Was Banished from Montenegro

WHEN BOYS FROM MAINLAND CITIES RUN AWAY FROM HOME, it's to see the sea. That's what they say when, shaking and remorseful, they confess at the first police station to which they're taken. Boys from coastal cities run away to go to sea, even if only as slaveys on fishing boats. It takes too much time and it's too unpleasant to stay in school long enough to get a master mariner's license. And besides, travel books give the impression that you can easily sail a ship on any sea, through any adventure, without bothering about a license. Some boys use running away as a kind of blackmail, to extort from agonized parents all the things they've wanted and have been denied. That's why we see the notices in daily papers of large cities that promise a Gino or Mario everything his heart desires. Just come home instantly—signed "your mother who is dying of unhappiness." But my decision to take a walking trip through the Balkans ten years ago with just a few crowns in my pocket, with a companion poorer than I whom I met by chance and knew only slightly, was made for a much more dismal and irremediable reason: to distract myself with physical fatigue, and new and picturesque sights, from an obsession, an internal anguish, which over a long period of time had become unbearable. I must, however, admit that I was a grown boy by then. In fact I was no longer a boy. I was about eighteen or nineteen years old.

So it was that on a brilliant morning (I don't recall anymore whether spring or autumn) my friend and I were at Cattaro, the last Austrian city on the Adriatic, ready to cross the mountains into Cettigne. We knew nothing about Cettigne except that it was the capital of small (small but impregnable) Montenegro. And the newly established relationship between the King of Italy and Prince Nicola[1] lured us into expecting a reception completely different from the one I am about to describe.

My companion (from the same part of country, if I recall correctly, as Fogazzaro[2]) had a card with him identifying him as a journalist for a provincial paper and a letter of introduction from a bishop. I had much less—a

---

[1]Nicola Petrovich, ruler of Montenegro. His daughter Elena married Italy's Victor Emmanuel to become queen of Italy.

[2]Antonio Fogazzaro, Italian author, native of Vincenza.

manuscript of poetry. Not knowing the route and not having a map, we needed to find someone to point the road out to us. We decided to ask a barber who was standing in the doorway of his just-opened shop, inside of which a boy was sweeping up. I told the barber what we needed to know, but instead of answering, he stared at us a long time with the intensely suspicious look of a primitive man guarding his cave, and while he stood there, the boy, broom in hand, hurried to his side to see the wonderful foreigners.

"I don't suppose you two are even Christians?" the barber finally said in as Croaticized an Italian as possible, with a kind of Dalmatian dialect. And then, "Not even Austrians?"

"No," I answered. "We're Italians, but I was born in Trieste."

The barber and the boy looked at each other for a long time, then at us, then at each other again.

A man who'd been walking slowly down the empty street stopped at that point to look at us too, and at our unexpected inquisitors.

"Do you want to take the new road or the old one?" the barber asked.

"Whichever is faster."

A long pause, heavy with mysterious deliberations, then, "Why don't you take the coach?"

"To save money," answered my companion.

But I made a quick correction. "Because we prefer walking."

"You're laborers?"

Something went through my mind about the various trades the other man could be in and warned me to slow down before I answered.

"No," I said, "we're journalists." But I'm sure the lie made me blush, because I knew that no newspapers were expecting articles from me. Besides, all I wrote then was poetry.

"Aha, journalists! And how much do journalists make a day?"

"It depends," I answered. "It depends on the paper they write for and on the work they do."

"You two, for example, how much do you make?" And his penetrating glance dropped to our feet to take in our walking shoes. Mine, at least, were new and passable. Then he looked over the rest of us with special attention to the quality and condition of our clothes.

"Please," he said, "turn around for a minute."

But we didn't turn around. Instead we made as if to move off. At that

point the barber's voice and gestures became unexpectedly cordial, almost
obsequious. He immediately gave us all the relevant information we required to keep from getting lost. He even offered to have his shop boy
accompany us to a certain crossroad, but we refused the offer because we
didn't need the help, also to save paying a tip. Finally, he dismissed us
with a bow and best wishes.

"Could he be a police spy?" I asked my companion when we were
some distance away.

"Why does he have to be a spy?"

"Didn't you hear all the questions? And the way he looked at us when
we said we were Italian?"

"He's Austrian," my friend said.

"And a barber," I added.

Shortly afterward we found ourselves on the slope of Mount Lovcen.

The walk from Cattaro to Cettigne took us almost the whole day. It
was only toward evening that, from a crest, we saw the gleaming red
roofs of the capital, roofs (it pleased me to think) so distant from Trieste's
and from my own house. The mountain air, the walking, and the charming
songs with which my companion eased our exertions had changed my
state of mind to one of peaceful excitement and aching sadness, which
was the ultimate goal of my trip, and enabled me to forget my long history
of unhappiness and to pretend (something I hadn't done for years) to the
deeds and feelings of heroes—to see myself as a Telemachus and my
companion as a Psisistrato, son of the wise Nestor, with whom, just as
light was fading from the road, I was arriving at an unknown city, the
seat of an all-powerful king.

While I was dreaming like that we could hear, almost as if to foster
my lovely illusions, the sad sound of a pastoral flute. When it stopped,
a young Montenegro boy dressed in native clothes approached us, followed
a short distance behind by his sheep. The Cettignian shepherd stared at
us the way the Cattaran barber had, but instead of the latter's suspicious
look, the boy had the joyful, embarrassed smile of an adolescent and a
way of walking that truly made me think of a prince of ancient days. He
greeted us, asked us quickly where we came from and where we were
going, then immediately afterward, as if it were the most important subject,
if we had much in the way of arms with us. When he heard that we didn't
have any (and it was the truth) he became unhappy, almost offended. He

couldn't understand why we would want to hide such nice things from him, who, as he explained in his own way, was crazy about them. Finally convinced more by his own hands, than by our words, that we really weren't armed, the boy drew out a very long double-barreled pistol, worn at his side in place of a dagger, for our admiration, assured us that he was a great shot, then apologized for not being able to prove the fact because he was out of ammunition. More than ten years have gone by since that evening, and I think now that the poor herdsman probably has had plenty of recent opportunities to prove his vaunted ability, if some hated Turk hasn't proven his own first.

As soon as he heard that we wanted to stay in Cettigne, and that we weren't planning to take lodgings at an inn, he invited us with great enthusiasm to stay at his father's house, even pointing it out to us. It was very close to where we were and yet outside the city. We accepted this (sad to say) as a good omen, and thus made our entrance into the capital of small (small but openhearted) Montenegro, followed by the young shepherd and by his not-in-the-least-innumerable flock. The head of the family being out, we were welcomed by the women. A multitude of women. And forget the Dalmatian barber! The curiosity these peasant women showed on seeing us reminded me of how the American aborigines reacted to their first sight of Christopher Columbus's sailors. There was no escape. They spoke a little Italian and every one of them wanted us to give her something, any kind of souvenir at all. On receiving it some of their embraces felt as hard as wood and some of their kisses seemed more like slaps and blows. With hands as dirty as they were greedy, and without our permission, they rummaged through all our bags. Piece by piece, snatching at one thing then another, they emptied them out, examined every single object furiously yet with minute precision, then suddenly pounced on something else. One woman wanted a button. I gave it to her. Then another clasped her hands together and asked for the faded, unbacked photograph of a friend.

Finally the young herdsman returned from looking after his sheep. With him was the old man who was head of the family. He shook our hands gravely, asked us to sit down, and after the usual polite remarks, and numerous observations and excuses about the poverty of his home, showed us a bed where, he said, one could sleep comfortably. As for food, he would arrange for us to eat separately. We told him no, there was no need for that, and that as a matter of fact, we preferred eating what everyone else did. Finally, thanking him for his hospitality, I asked what the cost of food and lodging would be per day. But he turned his head away, made a sweeping gesture as if to say that it was completely unnecessary to speak about such things, and that if we persisted, he would take offense. At that, out of fear of insulting him, and touched by so much cordiality and such unselfishness in a family that was so poor (poor but hospitable), I abandoned the idea of budgeting our expenses and in addition decided that I would never let these good people be out a single cent for us. They brought out wine, which we two nondrinkers barely tasted. After that the old man disappeared for a moment then came back with paper, pen, and an inkpot, looking like an innkeeper or landlord. However, he apologized profusely for the inquiries he made, saying they were not his idea but were required by law. In answer to the question about profession, my companion said he was a journalist. I simply gave myself the humble yet presumptuous title of "writer." We dined on a little leftover soup and goat cheese, then, asking our hosts' permission, immediately went to bed. But alas! There was so much and such restless life avid for our blood crawling around that bed, that fatigue notwithstanding, the women were already bustling around in the kitchen and the men working in the field, and we still hadn't fallen asleep.

We only stayed a few days at Cettigne. When the novelty had worn off, when we'd enjoyed the market, heard the lamenting Slavic melodies of certain old beggars, who accompanied themselves on single-stringed instruments while singing of expeditions and victories over the Turks and of their extraordinary national heroes (the like of which, they assured me, no other nation ever had or would have), the population, from prince to beggars, seemed replicas ad infinitum of the same Montenegrinos I'd seen in Trieste's taverns and cafés, who stopped at every table to offer patrons long, colored inlaid pipes, cigarette holders of fake amber, and other trinkets.

Then, too, my companion and I were not getting along well anymore. Among other things he was a fervent Catholic, as a matter of fact, almost an aggressive Catholic, who argued for the existence of God, while I, in turn, attacked him constantly and irrelevantly, denying it with every argument a fool of that age can muster when he wants to convince people, most of all himself, that there is no God. He was a strong believer in mother love, while I, perhaps to silence my own regrets, flaunted the greatest contempt for that kind of affection, declaring it too soft and effeminate. He told me about his conscience, troubled because a lovely young widow back home had gotten him to sin (he sinned, confessed, sinned again). And I laughed in his face and tried to make him see the absurdity of that God of his, who, after having created us in a certain way, would send us all off to hell for not being able to be different from the way He, in his omnipotence, had created us. This was the heart of our discussion, but the words then, of course, were quite different!

"You know," he said to me one day, listening to my blasphemies while sitting on a boulder, busily stripping the leaves from a branch with a penknife to make himself a walking stick, "I think it would be a good idea for us to separate. I'm going to Turkey and if you take my advice, you'll go back to your mother in Trieste."

Looking at him, I felt full of hate and, at the same time, like crying.

"All right," I said. "Of course, I won't go back to my mother in Trieste" (I did go back there a few days later) "but if separating is what you want, let's do it. And right away. In fact, the only reason I didn't suggest it first is because I was being kind."

My friend stood up without saying a word, while I, red in the face with my heart beating as if it would burst, resumed my assault on God with even more vehemence.

"It will be best," said my companion then, "to separate tonight."

"Let's go right down and pay the bill," I said.

Then I was silent to mull over a new suspicion. He's not in such a hurry (I thought) to leave me because he feels offended about religion but because he just discovered that I have less money than he thought I had. It was really an unjustified suspicion. However, it's true that he kept saying he was expecting a money order from home that never arrived. And in the meantime I was the one who'd had to pay our expenses.

Anyway, here's how I was banned from Montenegro. When, full of fear of offending our host, I asked him for the bill because we had decided to leave that very evening, the old man renewed his assertions of absolutely no interest in making a profit on us, seemed repelled at hearing our thanks, then drew out of a box an already completed bill that he presented to us with the air of someone who, if he accepts payment, is doing it only out of sensitivity to permit the other party the illusion that, with that small amount, he is completely absolved of any debt. Nevertheless, the sum was really enormous. For four nights on a hard, lice-infested pallet and meals worse than army food, the cost was higher than board and lodging would have been at a first-class inn, and not in Cettigne. I remember that the bill included the wine we didn't drink the evening of our happy arrival. And as for the soup, there was a separate accounting for every single kind of herb that went into its flavoring. A money-grubbing crook, in short, who instantly destroyed all my poorly conceived illusions about small (small but openhearted) Montenegro.

We expressed some reservations about the bill and our host's face darkened. We protested more energetically and the old man declared either we pay on the spot and up to the last cent or he would call the police. Perhaps he thought we were even more disreputable than we appeared and was using the threat as blackmail. However, we didn't let him scare us; in fact, we told him there was nothing we'd like better. In the meantime, those prying women came into the kitchen along with the shepherd who had reminded me of a prince. They all knew what was going on and stared at us with profound hostility. Everyone talked and shouted at the same time, and the women, standing a ways off, shook their fists at us. Then the old man said a few words to his subjects in their own language (perhaps warning them not to let us get away), and went out. He came back soon after with a police officer. The latter, already informed about the incident, asked to see the bill, and found it, he said, very modest. In fact, he ordered us to pay it.

"Not a penny more than half," said my companion.

At that point there was such an outbreak of anger around us—such lip clenching on the part of the old man, such fist shaking by the women— that I was already thinking of paying, just to get it over with, when the policeman asked us to come with him. At the police station to which we were taken, followed by the old man and the boy, they asked us, after we gave a brief explanation of what had happened, for our personal background, comparing it item for item with the facts they had. The interrogation went well for my friend, badly for me.

"Writer! What do you mean, writer?" asked the police officer, who strongly resembled his Austrian colleagues. " 'Whitewasher' is what you said last time, not writer."

And he showed me the paper, but it wasn't in Italian so I didn't understand a word.

"That's impossible," I answered. "The old man misunderstood me."

"Writer! And what did you come to Montenegro to write?"

"About the country," I answered.

My voice may have been bold, but one would have heard in it the desperation of vanity and a sense of literary shame.

The officer looked at me for a time, asked us both for our passports, then spoke to me again with indescribable contempt. "You! You want to write about Montenegro, when we've already had Mantegazza?"[3]

My friend's passport was in order, but I had only a certificate stating that I was an Italian national, with a marginal notation that read, "awaiting an official passport."

"Why," asked the officer, "don't you want to pay this bill?"

"It's not that we don't want to pay it. It's that we think it's far too high."

"They ate and slept in my house for five days," said the old man.

"Oh, how we slept!"

"I had the linen changed twice. And I want to be paid for it."

"I'm telling you again," I said. "We're ready to pay, but not at the rate of a crown for a plate of dishwater."

"All right," said the officer, "eighty percent. But you will both kindly leave Montenegro within twenty-four hours and never ever come back here again."

---

[3]Paolo Mantegazza (1831–1910), popular writer, particularly on scientific subjects.

God

1937

God

A MAN WAS TALKING TO HIS WIFE OF MANY YEARS and to his daughter, who was by then a young woman. They were talking about the meal the daughter would have to prepare that day because the mother, who was already dressed, was leaving for the country to visit some relatives on holiday. The man was proposing the summer meal that he'd loved best since childhood, rice in broth, boiled beef in tomato sauce, and if it was in season, eggplant in vinegar. But the mother was insisting that the daughter was incapable of putting together such a meal and that moreover she wouldn't know how to prepare the broth.

"All you have to do," the young woman told her, "is to show me once."

"Not once, not twice. You'll never learn."

The man intervened at that point. He told his wife that the deeper truth was that she was very jealous of her housewifely knowledge, and of the power that she derived from it, and that her resistance was a pretext so as not to lose even the smallest part of that power.

"If you only knew," she told him, "how happy I'd be to let it all go."

"You're only saying that because you want more. You'd give it all up, because you can't keep it all and have more."

"What wonderful character you have," the woman answered without much relevance, "and how ready you always are to take things in the nicest way possible."

"That's true, but only the smallest amount. And anyway you're not considering the suffering my imagination causes me."

"Yes, Papa," interrupted the young girl, who was or seemed this one time to be on her mother's side. "But your imagination is not what's under consideration today."

The man realized that the two women were basically right, that the character with which nature had endowed him was (could have been) good. And he decided that from that moment on, his life would be like this summer morning, in which he was speaking with his wife and daughter (his entire family) while sitting in front of an open dining room window, through which he could see the façade of a theater with a green tree next to it (the entire countryside) and the sky. He felt as if he were holding a brush in his hand, painting things that he had looked at for so many years for the first time. And in this fantasy he found happiness. Except that another idea occurred to him—that the fantasy was too lovely not to be hiding a snare. He saw that God, behind a white cloud that was expanding over the roof of the theater and thinning out so that some blue was perceptible at its edges, was watching him warily in order to destroy his happiness. And the little child in him was quick to become fearful and to renounce happiness for fear of punishment. Then another thought occurred to him—that the God who was watching from behind the white cloud was probably not at all the omnipotent Creator of heaven and earth, but a memory from his childhood (his beloved nursemaid), and the white cloud a half-open door.

Three Recollections of the Wondrous World

1946–1947

The Immaculate Man

NOW THAT I AM OLD I would like to write calmly and openly about the wondrous world, and to begin, as in fact I am beginning, with my recollections of Gabriele D'Annunzio.

I was just past twenty, and the bard just over forty, when I visited him for the first time at Versilia. His oldest son, Gabriellino, arranged for the visit—we were both living in Florence then—and, after receiving his father's telegraphed consent, brought me up to meet him. I hardly need say that this is something I had been pressing Gabriellino to do. And imagine! Of all the extraordinary things that my youthful foolishness encountered in Gabriele D'Annunzio's home, the one that's brightest in my memory today is a plate of pasta with tomatoes.

Summers in Trieste we ate pasta with tomatoes too. But our sauce's lovely color barely tinted the tagliatelle or spaghetti. Here it was over everything, right up to the rim of the plate that a servant, Rocco Pesce, famous in his own right, carried gravely around the table. The plate seemed a triumphal red banner and its rich flavor was superb.

I learned later that this was the way pasta with tomatoes was made throughout southern Italy and that Gabriele D'Annunzio's cook was indeed a southerner. But it was new to me at the time and I thought of it as a creation of the Image Maker. I even remember associating it with one of his poems. However, the other guests, who knew nothing of Trieste's cuisine, didn't share my astonishment. In fact, it was my astonishment that astonished them.

For many years now no one has been able to set my heart pounding the way it did when Gabriellino introduced me to the Glorious One. As I wrote in one of my "shortcuts," "no young man can consider himself well bred, by which I mean of a highly refined sensitivity, who, in the presence of a man of genius (or one so reputed) feels himself anything but a hatchling in an eagle's clutches. But," the shortcut adds, "perhaps this is a youthful recollection."

An immaculately white-suited gentleman greeted me, that is, a youthful-looking man dressed impeccably in white, who had a bewitching smile and knew how to use it. He was gracious to me from the first. Just how gracious I understand only now, because it is only now that I can imagine what a nuisance "that young poet," with his eccentricities and his (then fashionable) gray-blue frock coat with silk lapels, must have been. D'Annunzio excused himself from his son and other guests and led me into the garden of the villa, where he had me sit next to him on a bench. I can still hear the sound of the pine needles creaking under our feet. He asked me to recite some of my poems, that is, he said, if I wasn't too tired from my trip and if it wasn't too much of a bother. He admired or pretended to admire them. (Admiration was somewhat his specialty.) He said my poems had a great sweetness about them and that when he was my age (and here he sighed as if envious), he hadn't written anything as lovely, and that if I agreed to the idea he would recommend me to his editor. I agreed, almost with tears in my eyes. Later, I sent him a manuscript from Florence, which with doubts, irresolutions, and a variety of other insecurities cost me a month of agony. But the Great Forgetter neither answered nor ever returned that vexatious manuscript.

D'Annunzio was an indefatigable worker. If he weren't a great poet, one might call him a graphomaniac. Therefore none of his guests saw him except at meals. After dinner, however, he enjoyed being with us, but even so, he spoke very little and was content to leave conversation to others. Sometimes he'd have Wagner played on a mechanical piano called a pianola. (The pianola, as I learned much later, like all the appliances and furnishings in the house, as well as the house itself, was never paid for.) At the time D'Annunzio was working on a commemorative essay on Giacosa, who had recently died. I was amazed at his admiration for this "bourgeois" playwright and even more amazed when he made it quite clear to me that he didn't believe a single one of the complimentary words he'd written. But, he added, as if to excuse himself, Giacosa had been a dear friend, a perfect gentleman, and as he, D'Annunzio, wanted to do something nice for his widow, he was going to present her with this precious manuscript. He told me that the publication in which the essay was to appear had already paid him handsomely for it. "Before anything else," he said, contradicting one of his well-known maxims, "one has to live."

From there the conversation moved on to Italian literature. He spoke badly of Carducci, a little less so of Pascoli. He said that before himself, Italy had only three poets: Dante, Petrarch, and Leopardi; the others were nothing more than "balladeers." I agreed with his judgment, emphasizing "before him."

"My pride," he went on, visibly flattered, "is based solely on comparisons. No one is more humble than I before the immeasurable grandeur of art. It is only when I compare myself to other poets and writers, that I feel that I am a master." (His children were not permitted to call him papa in public, but had to call him "master.") I asked which of his poems was his favorite. "Perhaps," he said, " 'The Youth.' " At that time I liked his ode on the death of Verdi, and using local parlance, that is, a D'Annunzian turn of phrase, I said, "I know of someone who wrote a wonderful ode to Verdi, when he was actually thinking of Wagner." His answer to that youthful impertinence was a silence that seemed to last forever. But my remark wasn't only an impertinence, it was nonsense as well. He had been thinking of Verdi when he wrote the ode. My mistake became clear as I came to like Verdi's music more and more, and the ode less and less.

Staying with D'Annunzio, his sons didn't feel the same bliss or sense of continuous expectation that I did. Gabriellino was totally delighted when he announced that his father was giving us the following day "off." It was the day he was expecting his usual Thursday "visitor" and he didn't want us underfoot. Gabriellino showed me fifty lire—an enormous sum then—that D'Annunzio had given him so that we could have lunch and dinner at Forte dei Marmi, or anyplace else we preferred. "My father," Gabriellino observed ironically, "is always magnificent." And it was during that day off that the strangest of all the strange events of my visit to Gabriele D'Annunzio occurred: the voluntary sacrifice to the bard of a nonvital part of my anatomy, the blond goatee that like so many other males, young and old, I was wearing in those days.

For what it's worth, many people had noticed a certain resemblance between me and D'Annunzio. Perhaps the resemblance, if there was one, was due in large part to that beard and to baldness, total in the poet, well along in me. It seems that my host had noticed it too and that for obvious reasons he didn't like it. At least that's what Gabriellino led me to believe. "If you're really a good sport," he told me, "you'll cut off your beard (it doesn't look good on you, anyway) and give it to my father tomorrow. It will make him happy and he'll get your poetry published sooner." I gave in to the request, though reluctantly, and a Forte dei Marmi barber was entrusted with the simple task. When the poet saw me without the beard the next day he asked what had happened to it. Embarrassed, I handed him the remains in a white bag Gabriellino had given me. When he untied the bag and saw what was inside, he broke into loud laughter. Then, wanting to console me for my untimely baldness, which, alas, I couldn't undo even in homage to his, he said, "Only in perfect baldness is the perfect nobility of a head revealed. You and I have no reason to fear. But just think of a badly formed head, the prematurely bald head of some clod. Dreadful!"

The years passed and I never again had the pleasure of speaking with Gabriele D'Annunzio. One day, several months after my visit to Versilia, I saw him passing in an open cab through the Via dei Servi in Florence. It was early spring and the poet was wearing a violet in his buttonhole. I saw him one last time, during the war at Taliedo. How old he seemed! Just past fifty, he was already showing signs of that rapid, almost unnatural aging which would shock his visitors later on. The Hero was crossing the airfield followed by an attendant, a gigantic man, taller than the tallest of the king's cuirassiers, who like his boss was in nonregulation dress. As chance would have it, another of D'Annunzio's sons was my lieutenant. "Why don't you go and say hello to Father?" he offered, a little surprised at my lack of interest. "I'll take you up to him, if you like." But my brief D'Annunzian digression was over. What could I have said to him? Besides, I had recently discovered Nietzsche, although the Nietzsche I admired was different from D'Annunzio's, in fact, the perfect antithesis.

The only good things I salvaged from my D'Annunzian week were three poems from his *Autobiographia* (not among his most inspired) and a recipe for preparing that superb pasta with tomatoes. One winter afternoon in Trieste I was telling my young wife about them, and for her enlightenment made a point of praising the pasta and saying that I'd be very happy to have it for dinner that night. Considering the season, I had no doubt it was a futile desire. After that I went out, but when I returned, numbed by the cold and stunned by the wind, to our isolated house at the top of a hill, I found set out on the table in the pleasant warmth of our kitchen the same dark red marvel that had appeared seven years earlier on Gabriele D'Annunzio's board. The dish, made with a prepared tomato sauce called

Pancaldi, whose existence I hadn't known of, was again perfect. But this time I ate it with some sadness. The bard, debt-ridden, had emigrated to France. No important periodical had yet accepted any of my poems. No publisher had been willing to print my first "slim volume" even for money. Seven years. It wasn't much. But to me then, it seemed so very long, almost a lifetime. Because you have to understand, dear young reader, that in the distant days of my youth, youth exaggerated everything, even distances.

The Great Salvini and My Terrifying Uncle

"I KNEW YOUR NAME," I told him, "even before I knew the alphabet." I told him not only to please him but because it was true. Not that my family was overly in love with theatricals or was disposed to spend money on them, quite the contrary. One of the first times I went to the theater, as you'll hear, was to see and hear Tommaso Salvini; and by that time I was already twelve or thirteen years old. But a terrifying uncle of mine, who often had dinner with us, had in his youth been a volunteer with Garibaldi, and after that, he said, something like a secretary to Francesco Dominico Guerrazzi in Leghorn. Now he was in the business of buying and selling used furniture in the old part of Trieste. He was a good man— above all, as he put it, "a man." Nevertheless, even he had his foibles. One of these was to fulminate within his own four walls against "the laxness of morality"; another was to terrify pedestrians when, like Hippolytus, he drove skittish horses through the city streets. Whether the horses he bought were really skittish, that is, had faults that had been hidden from him, or whether (as dealers claimed to exculpate themselves) he wasn't an experienced enough driver, everyone was afraid of him and for him when, seated on the box of an elegant tilbury, he drove the high-strung animals Weininger considered symbols of madness through Trieste's crowded streets, dressed completely in white and seated next to (perhaps because of his love of contrasts) the only Black then living in my unsophisticated town, an Ethiopian whom my uncle with his substantial income had engaged as a servant.

This terrifying uncle had had frequent opportunities to appreciate Tommaso Salvini in Leghorn, and not only spoke of him often but even imitated his poses and the inflections of his voice. After a good fish dinner he would cheerfully condemn Achimelech to "a long and cruuuuu-el death." So when the newspapers announced that Salvini (who was quite old by then) would appear for the last time in Trieste in a special performance of Alfieri's *Orestes,* it was a foregone conclusion that my uncle wouldn't miss the event. Indeed, he didn't miss it, and kind uncle that he was, he took me along. However, he became unnerved at the box office. Four fiorini for two first-tier tickets! "That," he said, looking at me as if the fault were totally and exclusively mine, "is enough for a decent family to live on for four days." (It was true.)

The great Salvini undertook the part of Pilade, perhaps because it was less tiring, and with parental generosity left the role of the first hero to his son Gustavo. I remember little of the performance. Only a last act scene remains in my memory. I can see Tommaso Salvini almost as if I were still seated next to my Uncle Giuseppe in the gallery of the Fenice theater, making his grand fifth act entrance while Orestes, bloody sword in hand, exults in his recent triumph over his mortal enemy. The scene takes place in the Atridi palace, but there was nothing in the way of a stage set, the theater not yet having fallen into decadence. A pasteboard wall that shook at almost every step the actors took (and even without cause), the actors' talent, and Alfieri's poetry had to suffice, and they did. Pilade, big and bulky, his face partially hidden by a cloak, walked very slowly along that oscillating wall to speak to his friend, who is still unaware that he has killed not only his stepfather but also his mother.[1] "Give me that sword," he said. In his voice, in his step, in his glance now turned everywhere in fear, now stubbornly fixed on the ground, in every aspect of his manly and majestic figure, one read the horror of the news he carried but could not utter to the unhappy Orestes. Truly, those first words fell upon the audience as if they were hot drops of blood. I don't think it's possible to appear more dejected, more filled with dread and pity for a friend, more with terror for a matricide, more, in a word, the great, tragic actor. It's true that the situation warranted it, and that I felt my heart wrenched. Yet against all logic I seemed to be at home hearing my terrifying uncle thundering at the table against the laxness of morality.

That was the style of acting in a generation that has now passed. Unfortunately I didn't see, although I heard about, the prodigious two-and-a-half-meter leaps that Salvini took across the stage when as a young man he enacted Othello's jealousy, and the roarings of a wounded tiger craving revenge with which he responded to the evil Iago's insinuations. In his leaps and roars, as in his commanding presence and elegant style, he had no rival. Some, it is true, still preferred the memory of Gustavo Modena. They found him more refined, more poetic. He was so poetic that when,

---

[1]This is the thirteenth scene of the fifth act, the last in the play. In Alfieri's version of the *Oresteia*, Orestes, in his furious attack on Aegisthus, kills Clytemnestra unknowingly and unintentionally.

at a benefit, he would deliver a canto of the *Divine Comedy,* most often the third of the "Inferno," to his delirious public, he would appear before them dressed as the poet, that is, as Dante Alighieri (when Dante Alighieri dressed in red). Followed by a page he would pace the stage for a long while, clearly on the trail of some new and growing inspiration; then with an imperious gesture, he would point to a table and chair already in place, where the youth (really a young actress dressed as a boy) would sit and with a goose quill take down the immortal verses that seemed to issue spontaneously from the poet's brain. These things, of course, were told to me. And I have absolutely nothing to add. Nevertheless, those were blissful days. Because much of that roaring and posing, which died off in the theater, then passed—who would have expected it?—into our daily lives.[2] And there were many in that later audience who were obliged, though unwillingly, to pay dearly for their tickets of admission.

I met Tommaso Salvini in person in Florence at Trieste's Artists' Club, of which he was an honorary member. He was close to, if not already past, eighty, and had not performed for many years. We became, considering the enormous difference in our ages and the respect due someone of his renown, good friends. It was he who told me that often when he performed Hamlet on a Sunday afternoon in some provincial Tuscan town where hatred for the Austrian tyrant was most intense, he would have to raise the curtain after the play's conclusion. Hamlet's father's ghost would reappear and (whether by word or gesture he didn't say) revive the young prince. Without this happy mutation the people in the galleries would not have quieted down or left the theater feeling satisfied.

And when I gave a reading of my youthful poetry at the Artists' Club (my kind uncle had recently died after having predicted to my consternated family that if in spite of everything a good-for-nothing like me had a gift, the gift was—he didn't say it, but it would have been more correct to call it an affliction—for poetry), Salvini agreed to delay his usual billiard game that evening. (Despite his advanced age, he always won, though there were those who said they had to let him win.) Respectful as I was

---

[2]Saba is here referring to the rise of fascism, Mussolini's brand of which was heavily theatrical.

Libreria Antiquaria Umberto Saba in 1992.

Photo by Saul Gilson

Photograph of Umberto Saba as it appears in the bookshop.

of older people and of famous names "known before I knew the alphabet," prior to starting the reading I asked his pardon for my temerity in reciting in his presence. With what magnanimity he granted the expected pardon! Truly a sovereign deigning to please a subject. And when, at the end of the reading, I asked his opinion of my delivery, though approving, he offered two valuable criticisms. Unfortunately, I was never able to make use of the first; it concerned my unmistakable Triestine accent, for which I'd been banned by every radio station. But I've remembered the second at every opportunity. "One must," he told me, "always pronounce the last words of a speech in a louder voice, otherwise they will be lost to the audience." He liked one of my poems more than the others, one directed against Austria and the House of Hapsburg. Old patriot that he was, allied through the stage to Alfieri's poetry and the risorgimento, admirer of my city, which always greeted him triumphantly, he even deigned to interrupt the reading at a climax (a rhyme, may God forgive me, between "Hapsburg rule" and "cesspool") by clapping his glorious hands together, thus signaling the entire room to applaud.

My thoughts returned to Tommaso Salvini when just before the Ethiopian War I found myself in Leghorn. I wasn't there for pleasure but to buy a library being offered to my antiquarian bookshop. I was accompanied by faithful Carletto, acting, as usual, as superego. Even this famous employee of mine (now my associate) had, among his many virtues, several foibles. The greatest, perhaps, was that of never missing even the smallest opportunity to react to one of mine in a loud voice. (In other words, he was always snapping at me.) Leghorn, with its narrow streets around the naval academy, its tram then still pulled by horses, its nineteenth-century air, which reminded me of the Trieste of my childhood, made me feel I was tasting a drop of gold. And following the thread of one of my thoughts, I made it a point to stop and read every billboard in the street. Carletto, somewhat alarmed (it was already late for our appointment) asked me what I was seeking in the signs. "I'm looking," I told him, "for the program Tommaso Salvini is doing tonight, or better still, the one he's doing tomorrow, Sunday afternoon." Against all my expectations Carletto (who knew as well as I did that Tommaso Salvini had been dead for many years) didn't snap at me this time. He, too, loved Leghorn and for the same reasons I did. "Sometimes, Signor Saba," he said, "in spite of your dreadful character, it is a pleasure to be in your company."

And it was to Carletto, not to you, my late-arriving reader, that I first told these ancient tales at a trattoria, where I happily kept him company while he ate an extraordinary dish of tripe, charged against future profits. I told him about Tommaso Salvini and about my terrifying uncle Giuseppe; of how Giuseppe, a very tall man, had (and this, too, perhaps because of his love of contrast) a very tiny wife; truly tiny, with an angelic heart, though when it came to jealousy or love, truly fierce. So much so, that one day suspecting (probably incorrectly) that my good uncle was "keeping" two young women (sisters known throughout Trieste for their provocative charms), my aunt Gioconda stood up on a chair, made some excuse to get my uncle close to her, acted as if she wanted to stroke his pure white, patriarchal beard, and then as soon as she had it in hand, kicked away the chair and jumped to the floor with that prize still in her hand.

"Why," Carletto interrupted, "don't you write about these things? If you left out the names you might even get them published in newspapers and make some money without harming yourself or your family, much less the bookshop."

But in those days I neither wanted to nor was able to write for the papers. In those days, as good Carletto would often complain, I wrote only poetry.

Italo Svevo at the British Admiralty

VISITING MY OLD ANTIQUARIAN BOOKSTORE IN TRIESTE TODAY, I was once again struck by how much time and how many words it takes to close, or not close, even the smallest deal. When I arrived, the store's purchase of the *Children's Encyclopedia* was under discussion and the negotiations dragged on for at least another half hour to no avail. I remembered that in happier days (that is when it was I who was buying and selling), a "yes" or "no" was given more quickly.

I remembered, too, that about twenty years ago in the same place and on a similar occasion (endless negotiations between my stubborn assistant, Carletto, and an even more stubborn client), Italo Svevo told me, perhaps because of his love of contrasts, how things had gone with him in London when he closed the biggest deal of his life. A deal, I think, involving millions.

Italo Svevo (known in business as Ettore Schmitz) was a member of a Triestine firm that secretly manufactured and held exclusive rights for the sale of a mysterious product designed to protect the submerged parts of ships from the corrosive action of salt. The novelist, who by luck became famous just about the time he turned sixty, considered himself (and perhaps he was) a great businessman. I don't know if it was for that reason or because he knew English so well, but his firm gave him the responsibility of concluding negotiations already begun with the British Admiralty for its adoption of the celebrated underwater paint. This took place before the First World War when Trieste was Austrian and the English fleet was still enjoying its "Nelsonian" reputation. To the world, it was "the greatest naval force serving peace." For Trieste, every time the Mediterranean fleet anchored there peacefully, it meant festivities and guaranteed profits with, on the last night, fireworks on the wharves and from the great ships off the shore of that port of friendly trade. It was, to one and all, magical. Poor Schmitz, like everyone else, had fallen under the influence of that magic and climbed the steps of the austere Admiralty building with his heart pounding.

He was expected and was immediately taken into a small, cheerless, and bare room that was more the size of a closet than an office. How impoverished England seemed to him from the inside. After a few minutes a young man in street clothes appeared and offered him the only available chair. The official himself sat on the table, which together with the chair made up the room's total furnishings. He crossed his long legs, offered perfumed cigarettes and lit them for himself and his guest, showed himself to be informed on the matter, asked two or three questions, then announced that everything seemed all right and that the deal was essentially concluded. Italo Svevo thought he was dreaming. He had anticipated a long string of documents, one more boring than the other, and a series of interminable discussions. And here it took only five minutes for his cherished underwater paint to be adopted by the most powerful navy in the whole world. In Italy or even France, he said, it would have taken five years. When he left the Admiralty (although the deal was completely honest and, as all really good deals are, advantageous to both parties), he fell prey to a vague sense of guilt. Yet, at the same time, it seemed to him that his feet had grown wings.

He was a dear man, old Schmitz. After the specially printed praise of his novels, nothing pleased him as much as telling his friends stories of his long years in business. I heard more than one in the shop on the Via San Nicolò, where he used to drop in on me almost every evening, where the literati and (then) socially influential didn't disdain my conversation (if anything, the opposite applied), and which I visit as seldom as possible today. May God and good Carletto forgive me, but now all it is to me is a dark hole crowded with ghosts. The author of "Senility" and "The Confessions of Zeno" seemed to be, and was, full of humanity, of (relative) understanding of others, and after his unexpected literary success, of an affecting *joie de vivre*.

In reality, he had an enormous fear of dying. Whether it was a joke or some kind of premonition, he never got into a taxi without giving the driver a strange piece of advice. "Go slowly," he'd say in Triestine dialect, "you don't know who you've got in here." (Naturally, he was referring to himself, no matter who was along with him.) He died, precisely (and strangely), as a result of an automobile accident. He wasn't hurt badly but his heart, which was weak (he attributed the weakness to his abuse of tobacco), couldn't withstand the trauma.

But Italo Svevo was always a lucky man. No sooner did he understand that he was dying and that he had really smoked that "last cigarette," than his fear suddenly disappeared. "Is this all there is to dying?" he asked his family. "It's easy, very easy. It's easier," he said, trying to smile, "than writing a novel."

I've always thought (and these words uttered by that man at that moment confirm my belief) that humor is the highest form of kindness.

Motherhood

1947

Motherhood

LONG AGO, IN 1945, I lived in Rome for a few months, where I had, as a nostalgic line in one of my poems says, "Rome and happiness." It was a very fleeting and temporary happiness, as I was to learn quickly, built, as all happiness is, on the terrible sufferings of the past. But this of course, is of no concern, or hardly any concern, to a reader. Every day I'd go out to an arcade in the neighborhood of the Piazza del Popolo, where even then people were buying and selling all sorts of merchandise, to get a supply of Tuscan cigars, which I'd break up for my pipe, and without which my illusory happiness would immediately have turned into genuine anxiety. Sometimes I'd buy them from one woman, a blackmarketeer, sometimes from another. Eventually I always bought them from the same one.

Sitting among the competing vendors was a dark-complexioned, dark-haired woman, dressed in black, clearly a woman who'd come to Rome from the countryside. No longer very young, she carried a baby boy swathed in multicolored rags in her arms, on whom she bestowed an uninterrupted stream of blissful smiles. At times she would speak to him as if he could understand her. At times she would nurse him openly, without any false modesty. Very southern. Very simple and human . . .

One day she spoke to me. "Why, signore," she asked, "don't you get your Tuscan cigars from me every day?" And uttering those words, she looked around as if she were afraid of being overheard by her competitors. And then I saw her blushing, as though she were an honest woman driven by need to make her first less than honest proposal to a man.

From that day on I always bought my Tuscan cigars from her. It's true, I paid her a little more than I had paid the other women for them, but the difference was minimal and not that important to me at the time. I was fascinated by the woman and her child, by the intense, undivided love the poor woman showed for that tiny creature. How she looked at him! How she held him to her breast! The sweet words she murmured to him!

From time to time Allied Army patrols would pass by. It was always easy to tell when they were coming. Moreover, they'd be looking for their own country's cigarettes and tobacco and couldn't have cared less about Italian contraband. With the child in her arms, the woman would let them rummage through her things with quiet nonchalance, without ever uttering

a word of protest or cursing and abusing them under her breath the way
the other women did in their certainty, or at least under the illusion, of
not being understood. When the military police left, the woman would
turn her attention to the child again, would speak to him with increased
tenderness, as one does to someone dear after an escape from danger.

Things went smoothly for a while. Then one day the woman told me
she had no cigars left. The following day, and the day after that, she told
me the same thing. I looked at the upside-down orange crate that served
as her sales counter. There was nothing on it anymore. Nothing but a
pack of tissue paper and a lemon. A beautiful still life, but in no way
could it provide her with a living. What had happened? Had she used up
the capital she needed for business? Wouldn't anyone give her credit
anymore? In her face I saw, or at least thought I saw, if not hunger,
certainly signs of exhaustion. But there was no worry there, no sadness.
Didn't she still have her little boy?

I admired her and felt sorry for her at the same time. And one day
without even asking whether she had any Tuscan cigars (it was clear she
didn't), I put fifty lire in her hand. It was charity. The mother accepted
it saying, "Thank you, signore," not as though she were a supplicant, but
as if she were a lady collecting for charity, gratefully accepting whatever
monies came her way, to be used for the care of others. In this case,
others meant her child.

Eventually, I don't know how, things improved for her. Once more
the top of the orange crate was covered with new and different kinds of
merchandise, among them a few Tuscan cigars meant for me, which until
then she used to keep hidden in items of clothing. I was afraid that she
might try to return that wretched fifty lire to me. But she never said a
word about it. Instead, she reduced the price of the cigars to what her
competitors were charging.

After some time, I fled Rome and my temporary happiness, and never
again saw the woman or the little boy. But I remembered them suddenly
one day when a coldhearted Triestine friend of mine, a musician just back
from Rome (Triestinos are always, for reasons that I can't fathom, coldhearted, and musicians, for other reasons to do with their art, somewhat
foolish), inveighed in my presence about the brazen way in which the
black market was operating in Rome.

Lucky woman, I thought, and lucky little boy! Because there was one thing I was certain about. Whatever that boy's destiny in life (and it probably won't be very joyful), he would never fear dying of hunger. He might suffer it, but a soft and loving voice, the voice of his mother, who in 1945 for his sake was a blackmarketeer at the Piazza del Popolo in Rome, will remind him (without his ever being able to recall its long-forgotten origin) that "the saints always help."

And escaping jail by the skin of his teeth, if he is a believer, he will light a candle to the Madonna.

From Other Stories—Other Memories

1913–1957

Portrait of Bolaffio

I AM ALONE IN MY HOSTS' HOME. None of my friends is around. Some are at the shore, some in the country. And my longing for Trieste, to which I want so much to return, is centered in one person, someone who's been dead for more than twenty years: the painter Vittorio Bolaffio.

I don't want to judge his paintings. I am not an art critic like my friend Giuseppe Marchior, who suggested I write these pages. And anyway, what's the use of talking about paintings? You need to look at them. If it were possible to organize a retrospective of Bolaffio's work, of the few paintings he left that haven't been lost or destroyed by war or disaster, perhaps there would be ten or twelve people who, upon entering the gallery, would immediately perceive what a great, unknown painter Italy had after the First World War. A painter so anti–rhetorical that unlike the great Morandi, there was nothing in him of even the rhetoric of anti-rhetoricalism. But I'll be less pretentious and describe some strange aspects of his life, and some recollections of him (not all of them, however, because no one can ever tell everything about the living or the dead) that have remained dear to my heart.

Vittorio Bolaffio was born in Gorizia in 1883 or '84—I don't remember the exact year. Perhaps if he were still with us there would be a variation of a year one way or the other in his age. When I met him, he was closer to forty than to thirty. His physique (as Virgilio Giotti pointed out to me one day) was that of a musketeer, a D'Artagnan, but a D'Artagnan reduced to almost nothing. His face was small and triangular, his body extremely thin, and his clothes were so careless and shabby (not out of poverty; his father was a successful wholesaler of wine) that anyone would have happily exchanged them with a beggar's. And if you, dear reader, had offered him charity, I think that in humility—or whatever he mistook for humility—he would have cheerfully accepted it.

He was, alas! like almost all painters, foolish. But perhaps Vittorio Bolaffio was even more foolish than his average colleague. For example, he would spend entire nights with the Bible on one side of him and Lenin's writings on the other in order to study the texts and judge, he said, which of the two was the truth. Another example: Of all the fictional characters in world literature he chose as his favorite, without any doubts and without qualms, Jean Valjean. According to him, *Les Misérables* was the most beautiful and most "honest" book ever written. Strange affinity! Because even if Victor Hugo was from time to time a great poet, he was more consistently a great painter.

Bolaffio attended the Fattori school in Florence in his youth, then went to Paris. There, for a while, along with Modigliani, he lived what is called (or used to be called) "a Bohemian life." In between these two trips (to Florence and Paris) he took another, much more extraordinary one for that era, to India, which strongly influenced his art for the rest of his life.

This trip was undertaken, at least so he told his friends, as an act of conscience. It weighed heavily upon him to be financially dependent on his father and he was ashamed of not working.

He never considered painting work. This idea of physical work, which he looked upon as expiation and punishment, was an obsession (and not his only one) during his entire life. His most striking canvases are of men at work, mostly dockhands, bent and twisted under their heavy loads. So he decided to go to sea and signed up as a ship's stoker. Just the thing for his always precarious health! It's hard to understand how, but he was accepted. I think he might have paid for it. What is clear is that as soon as his father heard of Vittorio's weird new idea, he dashed down to see the captain of the ship armed with a bundle of bank notes called *corone* then in Trieste, which were as good as gold. He explained that his son was slightly off (not really crazy, and certainly not dangerous) and begged the captain in God's name not to tell his son anything of his visit, but to accept under the circumstances payment for round-trip, first-class passage, plus a little extra for his trouble. They were to let Vittorio work for a few days in the engine room, but at the first sign of fatigue, he was to be sent to sick bay and ordered to complete the voyage in a comfortable cabin. And indeed, that's the way it happened. There's no way of knowing how much time young Bolaffio spent in the hellish engine room and how much resting in a cabin. But that trip and seaboard life left an indelible impression on him. There were notebooks upon notebooks (in reality small, grimy memo books bound in red) in which, in the cafés, taverns, and more wretched places where he spent his dismal existence, he drew, crossed out, sketched and resketched, with the desperate intensity of an obsessive, all the visual memories of his voyage from Trieste to Bombay and back. They were supposed to be part of an immense triptych that he dreamed of reproducing on the walls of some Triestine tavern. He even found the place he thought best suited for it, a popular and prosperous tavern along the shore front. He began eating there regularly, planning at each meal to explain his idea to the owner of the place. But so great was his fear of a refusal that time after time he lacked the courage. The day he finally worked up the nerve to do it, the owner told him (courteously, he didn't want to lose a customer) and not exactly in these words, that his tavern's walls were just fine bare and didn't need to be frescoed. But Vittorio Bolaffio wasn't discouraged. He decided to buy, or to be more precise, to have his father buy, the place. Being a vintner, his father also considered it a good idea. But good or bad, nothing further came of it. And nothing more remains of Vittorio Bolaffio's voyage to India than two or three canvases (if they still exist), scattered here and there. Bright and luminous!

Perhaps this little story has given you some idea of the man. But there are so many others I can tell! There's one about another trip, a short one from Gorizia to Trieste during which a man with another strange occupation (he was an agent provocateur) got him to sound off against Mussolini; then afterward, pretending an excess of patriotic indignation, he took him down to police headquarters. Friends and family passed him off as incompetent and eventually he was released. The first evening that he went back to the café where he usually met his few friends, they expected to find him dispirited. Not in the least. The only thing that had impressed him about prison were the jailers. They were, he said, the real prisoners, the true victims of the system. It was necessary to help them, to send them money. And probably that's what he did.

Kind and generous as few are, he was nevertheless in spirit, as in body, somewhat a musketeer. One time at the café, he slapped a waiter. I can't remember why. Then he was sorry, and when the waiter lost his job for unrelated reasons, Bolaffio always asked him to eat with him. As a matter of fact, whenever a friend used to meet him at the trattoria, there at a nearby table would be the waiter, slapped once and fed forever.

Fascism shocked him. There is a large painting, in fact two variations of the same painting, that he would have liked to call "Speaking of Mussolini." There are two men in it, a youth and an old man (probably his father; all the old men he painted resembled his father, even that wonderful captain mounting the bridge of one of those steamships that used to ply the coastal route between Trieste and the Istrian towns, who, bent and with his hands crossed behind his back, looks exactly like one of Conrad's ruined captains). The two are sitting on a red bench in a public garden. The old man has a newspaper spread across his knees. The youth, clearly a socialist, with a red carnation in his buttonhole, and his legs crossed, appears to be speaking forcefully and with great conviction. It could be a genre painting. But it is one of the great things in contemporary Italian art, not because of, but in spite of its imprudence and some apparent technical deficiencies. Critics and art lovers were inhibited by these. Few saw that beyond such tactlessness there is a profound accomplishment. In Paris they would (perhaps) have understood. In Trieste . . .

At about the age of forty, Bolaffio became ill with tuberculosis of the larynx. It was, for a man no longer at a susceptible age and not without means, a curable illness. The way he dealt with it meant suicide. The doctor who was taking care of him guaranteed his recovery. All he had to do was spend a year in a sanatorium or at the shore. Bolaffio went to live in a furnished room in one of the unhealthiest parts of Trieste, with a nice, opportunistic family who, with the excuse that they were risking contagion, charged him more for their hospitality than he would have paid in a first-class sanatorium. There was no need, however, to spur him on in this. When one of the young girls in the family went out to get him a bottle of beer, Bolaffio gave her a hundred (old) lire and never asked for change. A sin, perhaps, but its opposite, greed, is much uglier!

He, who painted with extreme difficulty, and who, when face to face with a canvas, would add a brush stroke every quarter of an hour, couldn't bear hearing compliments about his work. One evening, at his usual café, a young man walked up to him and, calling him "master," told him his work was avant-garde. (Young painters have always had a fixation on the avant-garde, almost as if art were a battle and its only purpose was to irritate and outrage.) Vittorio Bolaffio rose to his full height and shouted at the top of his lungs that his place was in the rearguard, in the furthest imaginable rearguard of painting. Perhaps it was a disguised form of pride, but the young avant-gardist hurried off (saying good-bye like the good-hearted boy he undoubtedly was with a nice fascist salute), and was never seen again. Bolaffio began to tolerate, even to want, praise only during his last illness, almost as if his art had been a sin (he certainly felt it as such), and the imminence of death required absolution. He became attached then to the few paintings he had completed with so much anguish and pain. He had those which had been sold (?) or given to friends brought into his sick room. He would gaze at them tenderly for long periods of time and say, "Yes, they are beautiful, really beautiful." And he charged a young painter who was helping him (not the avant-gardist) with the responsibility of making photographic reproductions of them. He knew he was dying and was happy for it. In a weak voice, he praised life's sweetness, the wonderful goodness of friendships, and morphine, which relieved his last episodes of choking. A deathbed is a deathbed, but I don't recall ever witnessing a dying as peaceful as his. The obsessions that had tortured him during the course of his life seemed to have resolved themselves into a kind of overwhelming bliss.

Just before his last days I had to make a trip out of the country. We both knew that we would never see each other again, but neither of us spoke about our nearing eternal separation. I said good-bye to him as I always did, as if I would see him later that evening at the café, but I saw tears in his eyes. So I took his hand and said, "Allow me to kiss a hand that has painted such wonderful things." He wanted to protest but was too weak. When I returned home, as I'd expected, he was dead. I was barely in time to attend his funeral, a funeral, according to his wishes, of the cheapest kind. The funeral of a pauper.

He was, the reader will have understood, a strange man. But enough said, he was a man.

Five Anecdotes with One Moral

THE CLIMATE OF AN ERA is derived not only from its so-called major historical events. An insightful person can know it, without even seeking it, from small clues in everyday life.

During the Munich era I was in Paris. I had to get to a small suburban inn to meet a friend. A Frenchwoman accompanied me. My "guiding star" led me into the lobby of the hotel just at the moment the radio was broadcasting a speech by Hitler. The proprietor's daughter, a young German Alsatian, came bounding out from behind the counter, shouting as though possessed, "Spricht Hitler. Spricht Hitler." Her eyes were sparkling with love for Hitler and with hate for all that wasn't Hitler. And her quivering body seemed attracted to the magnetic energy in that beloved, oh so human voice. I turned to see how my companion, who knew enough German to understand that "spricht Hitler" meant "Hitler is speaking," would respond. She had such a lovely French name and had often declared herself a mortal enemy of the "Boches" and their intelligent theories. To my great surprise, there was no response. What there was instead was a charming smile with which she sought to disarm Hitler's lover before asking, almost humbly, if the person we were seeking was "à la maison." From that smile I knew that the Maginot line had been a large and useless expense, that the "Boches" would have no trouble invading France, and that once there, they would find many willing collaborators. And I decided to return to Italy.

When I was young and even after that, until sometime after the First World War, if two dogs, one large, and the other small, were fighting in the streets (one trying to eat, the second to castrate, his adversary), everyone's sympathy was always with the courageous little dog. It was a way of showing oneself to be Garibaldian.[1] That this behavior was about to change, or had already changed, was a lesson I learned from an incident early in 1938 in the Viale XX Settembre in Trieste. A shepherd and a Scotch terrier—to see each other was to hate each other—were (because of failed muzzles) battling in the street. From the circle of spectators that

---

[1]Garibaldi was the dashing hero of Italy's reunification, much loved by the "common man."

formed quickly around them came shouts directed toward the large beast, "Get him, go get him." This warmhearted incitement came from a group of boys who would have been better advised in their own self-interest to be on David's side against Goliath. But their shouts told me that should Belgium be invaded again in a second war, Europe's youth would no longer feel any moral obligation to defend the weak. The end had come for small countries. They would be swallowed up by the large, "Nazionalized."

During a cold, snowy day in the same era, I found myself on a tram. The car was so crowded that it was difficult for me to pay for my ticket. But to walk through the crowds that blocked the narrow aisle, to get off through an exit prescribed by regulations, was an undertaking beyond my or, in my opinion, anyone else's power. I decided then to make a virtue of necessity and get off from the rear running board. In an earlier age, passengers either wouldn't have paid any attention to me or would have quietly helped me. They would have, I think, identified with me. In the climate of fascism, they identified instead with the ticket taker, who in turn was identified with Mussolini. After vain attempts to restrain me by holding my arm, several of the more zealous actually got off the car to try to stop me and force me to get back on. (I still remember—if not with joy, at least not with too much remorse—that one of my persecutors took a bad fall on a sheet of ice.) It's very possible that even these people were, in their secret hearts, antifascists, but as a crowd, dictatorship had contaminated them. They didn't allow each other any exceptions from the rule, whether for love, fear, or both simultaneously. Nor did they allow exceptions—even for circumstances beyond anyone's control, or for issues as inconsequential as this was to anyone else. "Why you and not me? Who do you think you are?"

Boys have always played at the seashore or wherever else they find running water, diving, splashing, or wrestling each other. But these were always individual activities. A boy would jump on his friend's back and the two would tumble together along the sand or grass. Walking along the Tiber in 1945, however, I came across an unexpected variant of the old games. In this, individuals had become a collective. Every few minutes another boy would come dashing up, only to disappear immediately amid the others into the brawling mess. They had become an immense human polypod, a beast, thrusting and waving its tentacles—arms and legs impossible to assign to a particular body—in the air. Punches and blows went this way and that. People watching them from the famous shore were enjoying themselves (or at least they seemed to be). They were enjoying the spectacle of the new generation losing its sense of individuality and developing, even in games, a taste for forming part of an ever-larger mass.

A few days ago, in a bar in the Piazza Caiazzo in Milan, two young patrons wanted to rent the billiard table for their daily game. The owner told them that this time, he couldn't let them play. He had just replaced the cloth. "If either of you tears it," he said to the two, "how will I ever get my money back? Do I know your names? And even if I did, could I get the thirty or forty thousand lire out of you that it cost me?" The barkeeper was justified. But what astonished me this time, even granting he was right, was the lack of any response on the part of the boys, the passivity with which the two of them accepted the pronouncement. They made no attempt, as my generation certainly would have, to argue. They didn't even plead. They looked at each other for a moment, as though a little (but not too) chagrined, and walked out.

Whatever judgment one may have formed about these younger people, it is certain that insofar as they have moved away from "neuroses" they have moved closer to accepting reality. But neurosis was a defense, a bulwark—against insanity, for example, and against criminality. And it occurred to me that the counterpart to the two good boys of the Piazza Caiazzo can be found in their unfortunate cohort from Vetriolo.

He was a youth of about twenty, whose name I don't recall. He shot his entire family to death (except his sister) in broad daylight, and I think several other people as well (though not intentionally). It was one of those monstrous crimes which seem to make no sense, but which trail after long wars like the tail of a comet. He was condemned to prison, "to" (as the expression went at one time) "eat the bread of affliction, and drink the waters of sorrow for the rest of his days." Wouldn't it have been simpler, more (if the word still has any meaning) humane, more, if you will, economical, to have, after offering him the obligatory religious and civil comforts, employed one of the many forms of euthanasia science has at its disposal today? I fear that Cesare Beccaria[2] was fooling himself when he diminished the severity of the law by substituting life imprisonment for the death penalty; and that the great jurist may indeed have been a sensitive man, but that he was lacking a little in—how to say it?—imagination. Even for its intimidating effect, men (always because of this lack of imagination) fear death (even without pain) more than . . . anything else.

---

[2]Italian jurist and criminologist (1738–94) who deplored torture and capital punishment. His major work, *Of Crime and Punishment,* influenced penal law throughout Europe.

A Pistol Shot

TRIESTE WAS AS WELL KNOWN FOR ITS CITY CAFÉS as it was for its country-side taverns. The cafés that came to it from Vienna were slowly crowded out by bars "imported" from America. The few remaining cafés are like old nineteenth-century gentlemen living in a world that is becoming more incomprehensible to them every day. The taverns, on the other hand, have remained essentially the same. The pistol was fired one recent evening in one of those suburban taverns.

A young American soldier turned up at the place. There were numerous customers inside discussing high politics. After having paused for a moment on the threshold, the soldier entered the tavern, took a pistol from his pocket, and shot it into the air. Poor boy! Far from his homeland, in a city and among surroundings that were unfamiliar to him, he nevertheless had to find some way to affirm his own existence, to say—here I am, living in this world too! He didn't speak Italian, he was used to different customs and manners and had only that strange means at his disposal to convince himself and others of a reality that though insignificant to them was of utmost importance to himself. He couldn't attract the least attention to himself by writing "The Raven," (as his countryman Poe had done) or by succeeding at some wonderful undertaking. Unable to fascinate, he hoped at least to frighten. Thus a people that felt itself unloved provoked a catastrophe; thus a child will set off a firecracker under your feet.

The act could have had serious consequences. Trieste isn't by any means the Far West one admires at the movies, and its atmosphere these days isn't the breezy one that surrounds cowboys. Everything here is very different, and the young soldier (for whom, perhaps, that tavern had not been the first stop on a round of drinking) seemed suddenly aware that he had committed a tactless act. But as he couldn't now take it back, he stood his ground bravely and waited for a reaction. What he seemed to be saying was, "If anyone has any complaints to make, let him come forward." No one had any complaints (or so it appeared) and no one came forward. Instead cheers broke out, shouts of bravo, great, encore, accompanied by laughter and applause. It was as if instead of shooting off a firearm, he had emitted some extraordinary and surprising sound like a high C. Disconcerted by the unexpected reception, which seemed to be encouraging him to continue, the soldier's face darkened. He put the gun back in his pocket and, mortified, left the tavern without saying a word.

We weren't eyewitnesses to this event. I reported it, having heard it from a skilled worker employed at Riuniti. Even before he had finished speaking, however, my thoughts had gone back in time to the memory of an analogous episode in the life of a dog named Occo, which—in order to extract an improbable and unwonted moral—I'm going to take the risk of telling you about now.

Occo the dog was a fervent enemy of cats, who, as far as he was concerned, represented all the evil on the face of the earth. Twenty or thirty years ago that enmity was a daily entertainment in the streets. Today, either because of the dangerous growth of traffic, which makes it necessary to keep dogs on leads, or because the people who worry about those things have found ways to ease the traffic with straighter roads, the spectacle has become rare. But in those days, Occo the dog couldn't bear to see a cat without flinging himself at it. The poor beast was too dumb to understand that impeded by his muzzle, all he could do was chase cats. No way could he really destroy them. By a stroke of luck the cats were just as dumb as he was, and whenever they saw him come toward them in that state of fury, they climbed up a tree or ran to hide inside something. However, there once was—and only once—an extraordinary cat, a cat out of a book of fables, who neither fled nor seemed disposed to confront her terrible enemy. Seated quietly in the doorway of a grocery store, she responded to his provocation in almost the same way the customers in the suburban tavern had responded to the pistol shot. She didn't arch her back. She didn't swell her tail. She didn't hiss in his face. She looked at him (we don't know how else to describe it) with a kind of ineffable smile. Occo, to whom such a thing had never before happened and to whom it would never again happen, behaved in turn like the young soldier from the Far West. Even better, because instead of leaving the site mortified, he turned around and happily wagged his tail. We have before us as strong as possible a living demonstration of a precept of the far-off Buddha. "Enmity," it says, "doesn't end enmity. Friendship ends enmity."

Royalty

DEAR REPUBLICAN READER, don't be alarmed. The old man here writing his memories of a world he persists in recalling as wondrous doesn't want or fear a return to monarchy any more than you do. But, brought up under Austria's Franz Joseph, whom he (mistakenly) hated, in his early days he longed for an Italian king—more precisely, for an Italian king in Trieste.

They told many stories then about the young king. They said that he was a socialist at heart and had cheerfully declared, "I would have no problem calling myself Mr. Savoy in a republican Italy." They also said he was well informed on every subject, though less so in the arts. This limitation toned down my enthusiasm a bit. Irredeemably a poet, I would have preferred a king who could have liked my poetry. But where do you find such? A queen, perhaps, but a king . . .

I saw him close up only once, at the airfield in Taliedo. It was the spring or summer of 1918. The danger of a German invasion of Lombardy had barely been averted at Montello. He seemed cheerful. He accepted the huge bouquet of red roses that a Caproni employee[1] offered him as he reentered his car with what I would say was sincere appreciation. I liked the simplicity and austerity of his style and that of his small entourage, much more so when I compare it to Gabriele D'Annunzio's pomposity. The bard had also visited the air base, and compared with the king, he was a boor. He was wearing a cavalry uniform (the branch in which he had served in his youth) with its white collar so extremely high that it hid half his face, which made him seem older than he really was. His aide, also in nonregulation dress, to which he had added every possible embellishment, was a giant of a man, chosen by the poet for his fearful appearance. The king's aide could have been any infantryman whatsover, a man from Corso or from Montello, someone who would join his company in singing the popular song in which a captain orders his men to cut his body in four (or seven) pieces after he dies, and to offer the first of them to the king of Italy, "so that he may remember his soldier." That's because the soldiers who fought in the earlier war more or less loved him, all of them; perhaps even those who were court-martialed, sentenced to death, and who faced the firing squad (the wondrous world is truly too full of blood

---

[1] Caproni was Italy's premier aircraft, named for its designer, Giuseppe Caproni.

and tears) shouting an inversion of their oath: "Down with the king and his royal successors." And in the end, we need to remember, for him, for ourselves, for everyone, what old Shakespeare had another king say, and an old king at that. "There are no guilty people, just unfortunate ones," Lear says to his daughter Cordelia in prison.[2] And for that sentence alone—consideration of their poetry aside—I love Shakespeare even more than Dante.

At about the same time and at the same place, I also saw the crown prince. Physically very different from his father, he appeared to be too conscious of his glamour and of his exalted status. Smiling at everyone and everything, he was in essence smiling only at himself.

When I was an antiquarian book dealer in that dark shop at Via San Nicolò 30 in Trieste, from time to time I'd have the pleasure of a visit from Anna of France, the young Duchess of Aosta. My pleasure derived from her person, not her purchases; the books she bought from me were nothing special. She, on the other hand, was enchanting. Perhaps it was merely a matter of etiquette, but even etiquette, carried to that degree, has poetic and human meaning. I was moved by the uncertainty of her destiny (which I foresaw), by the elegance of her bearing and dress, and the perfection of her hands, hands which

> required two thousand years
> of French history to produce.

But more than anything else, I was struck (perhaps erroneously) by something she did. Leaving the shop one day, and already at the door, she made the then obligatory parting gesture that seemed almost unsuitable for women. I, who didn't know how to return that salutation, bowed instead. Anna of France, or just Anna, as everyone called her, walked back a little ways and with a smile offered me her hand. Most likely it was nothing more than a woman's intuitive act, but to me it seemed (and I couldn't be sure that it wasn't) something more, a kind of discreet and

---

[2]This is a translation of the quotation as it appears in the Italian. Saba seems to remember what he chooses to remember. There is no such line in the prison scene between Cordelia and Lear.

silent affirmation of my feelings. I was grateful to her then, and (as the reader can see) I am still grateful.

The last royal personnage I met belongs, if not to another world, to another family. During the last catastrophe, a young duke who was a member of England's royal family was serving in his country's army. He held the rank of captain but his identity was unknown as he used a fictitious name. I met him in Florence in 1944 and again in Rome in 1945. In those days it was difficult, if not impossible, to communicate between the two cities. And I, who had just gotten to Rome by a stroke of luck, wanted to reassure my wife, who had stayed behind in Florence. To do this, I got in touch with an English friend at the PWB[3] and requested that he ask the first soldier he ran into who was headed for Florence on official business to take a letter to my wife.

"Your wife," the duke told me at dinner a few days later, "is a very kind woman. When I gave her your letter, she immediately offered me a glass of wine, and before I left, she gave me fifty lire." I must say in my wife's defense that the poor woman doesn't see well, that the house she was living was quite dark, and that (anonymity apart) she has never, in all her long life, learned to distinguish military ranks. For all these reasons she confused the illustrious bearer of my letter with an ordinary Allied soldier, who, she assumed, like any soldier the world over, relished no pleasures more than a drink and a tip. And judging from the tone in which the Duke of Norfolk told me the story, I'd say he'd relished them too. Perhaps they were even a greater pleasure for him. Or at least, a rarer one.

---

[3]Psychological Warfare Branch—Allied military forces office for war propaganda.

The Story of a Bookshop

NOW THAT I AM OLD I would like to write calmly and openly about the wondrous world; and among other things, the dark shop I had at Via San Nicolò 30 in Trieste, which my friend, Nello Stock, who loved the place and whiled away countless hours in it, called, and with good reason, "the shop of miracles."

Walking through the Via San Nicolò one morning in 1919, I saw or noticed that gloomy cave for the first time and thought, "What a sad thing it would be to have to spend my life in there." It was, although I couldn't know it then, a warning or a premonition, because a few days later I bought just that store from its owner, old Giuseppe Mailender. I bought it intending to throw all the old books in it into the Adriatic and to sell it empty at a higher price. (Everyone was looking to buy a shop then in Trieste.) But after a few days, I didn't have the heart to carry out the plan. Even though their contents didn't interest me in the least, the old books had enchanted me. I was also trying to find a way to earn a living. I wrote to my wife, who was spending the summer in Portorose, to tell her what happened and ask her advice. She wired back, "Don't sell the bookshop." It made me think of one of Sancho Panza's sayings, "A wife's advice is not much as a rule. But he who doesn't heed it is surely a fool." I heeded her advice. And that's how I came to spend almost half my life in that gloomy cave. Part of the time in it was good and part bad, just as, I suppose, it would have been in any other place. But the shop on the Via San Nicolò had one great merit. During all the years of fascism it was a refuge, sheltering me from loudspeakers. It's fairly hopeless for a poet to make a living in literature. And during those years it seemed more hopeless than ever. However, the antiquarian books, whose existence I'd just discovered, didn't upset me or reflect the hateful face of the present, the way almost all of the new ones seemed to do. What's more they gave off a sense of peace, as though they were the honorable dead. I'm still not sure whether I really loved them. Perhaps I did, but in a peculiar way—the way procurers love beautiful women, to sell them.

I knew nothing about antiquarian books. All I knew was that there were books called incunables, and that Aldo Manutius had been a great sixteenth-century printer. Nevertheless, I don't think I ever made a really bad purchase, or that I ever caused any of my customers to do so. A kind of instinct guided me from the first moment. I don't know if there was anything exalted about the instinct, but anyway, I don't intend to boast about it. I took my first steps under the guidance, or rather, under the wing, of Tammaro De Marinis. I was visiting some friends in Florence, when one of them, a lawyer whose office was in the building in which De Marinis had his shop, offered to introduce me to him, warning me, however, not to buy anything from that scheming old fox (he used another word). I had very little money and a great fear of losing it. Alone with De Marinis, he asked me if I wanted to see any books. I said I'd be happy to. From a magnificent showcase, the eminent antiquarian produced a sixteenth-century Ovid with elegant engravings. I asked him how much it cost. "One hundred lire," he said. With my heart pounding a bit, I bought it. Then he took another sixteenth-century book with engravings from the same shelf, an extremely rare Hebrew Aesop. I asked the price: eighteen hundred lire. I told him it was too high (in reality I had absolutely no idea whether it was high or not). When I turned it down, De Marinis took out other books. Some I bought, some I didn't. Finally, after showing me an expensive incunable that he said cost two thousand lire, and which I'd declined, he told me the book was worth twenty thousand and that he had offered it to me at that price because he had begun to suspect that I knew nothing at all about antiquarian books. He said it in a very courteous way and with great tact. And I, who by then had begun to appreciate Nietzsche's aphorism, "I sit in the arcade asking passersby, 'Who wants to cheat me?' so as not to have to guard myself against deceivers," confessed he was right. Besides, I'd had the feeling that De Marinis was a man of integrity and wouldn't take advantage of my ignorance. "In that case," he replied, "leave everything to me. Trust me. If you don't sell the books you buy from me, I'll take them back. I'll even put it in writing, if you want." I accepted his terms and bought about ten books for around a thousand lire.

When I saw my friend again and told him what had happened, he looked at me pityingly and asked how I could possibly think I'd make a profit selling books bought from (according to him) the most expensive antiquarian book dealer in Italy. (He was all wrong. And I want to make it clear for the information of anyone who may follow me into the profession, that the best deals I made were always with the most eminent antiquarians.)

Back in Trieste I had my share of anxieties, but within a month I'd resold all those books at a substantial profit. The first thing I did was go back to Florence, to Marinis again, where I bought more books more courageously. But I couldn't afford to go beyond a certain amount, and I told him that. That's when he offered to give me everything I wanted on consignment. He would set the prices he wanted, which I'd then be able to raise, he said, almost double. I was moved by his trust in me.

Every two months or so, he would ship one or two crates of strange books to me in Trieste with variations in price that I could never comprehend. Even though I didn't send out catalogues at the time, I managed to sell almost all of them; and he never took advantage of me. It was I who took advantage of him. This is how it went. By degrees, as I sold a book I would pay him, except for one or two (often the most expensive). When I got to the end of the shipment, I would tell him that a certain number of books were unsold (among them those that had been sold, but had not yet been paid for), and that if he didn't want them back I would buy the remaining lot at half his original price. He almost always accepted, adding very little to his asking price. I think he added the small sum to discourage me from doing it too often. The truth is that many of those books which were relatively inexpensive were something of a discard for De Marinis, and perhaps it wasn't a matter of his not liking them, but of ridding himself of them. He was already dealing at the highest levels of bibliophilia. Shortly thereafter, in fact, he closed his shop, turned up the Este Bible, and became a star on the international bibliophilic scene.

I don't think he had any personal feeling for me, in contrast to, and I am pleased to acknowledge it here, his "competitor" and my very kind friend, Mario Armanni. I bought many books from Armanni, too, over the many years. But he had a certain affection for my poetry, and I think—may the Lord forgive me—that I even exploited that affection. But one has to make a living. De Marinis and later Armanni were the principal suppliers of my little bookshop for many years. Both were from Naples and both great gentlemen, as southerners are, when they are. It was wonderful to see them together. I was at one of their business meetings once. They treated each other with great respect and a moderate formality. Their discussions reminded me of those between the curate and the count in Manzoni's *The Betrothed*.

Meatballs in Tomato Sauce

DEAR LINUCCIA, who's been gone for such a long time from what was once our home. You're asking me about the ingredients—about what basically went into the famous meatballs in tomato sauce that your mother used to make. If I told you it was love, I wouldn't be telling you anything new. The truth is, I don't know what else to say. But your question reminds me of two happenings, of two invitations we extended—the first, connected to the meatballs in tomato sauce, the second, as you'll see, much more exotic.

Your mother, who wasn't a literary person, and who spent two-thirds of her life in the kitchen preparing meals for those she loved, which, though limited in variety, gave off the same glowing warmth and derived from the same core of deep feelings (the unmistakable mark of a way of life and, therefore, of a style), found relief, so to speak, in making meatballs after you left to pursue your own life, and our house became the home of two wretched old people—each trying to hide from the other the selfish desire to be the first to die, so as not to be left alone on this earth. We didn't send out invitations anymore—except for the two I'm going to tell you about in this letter, which, if you like, you could even consider a new, alas! and belated memory-story.

The meatballs with tomato sauce, which neither you nor I will ever again taste in this world, though always prepared in the same way were served in two different ways. Your poor, departed mother ate them warm and without sauce. I ate them cold in a dish filled to the brim with tomato sauce. With this in mind, the minute they were done, I'd put six or seven aside, pour the sauce over them, and carry them into the dining room to cool off. Now, it so happened that Noretta, that friend of mine, who—and this is your description—if she'd been a bird, would have been a falcon, came to see me at home one day.[1] It was, I think, about eleven o'clock in the morning. Seeing that dish, which was quite appetizing in appearance as well, she couldn't resist temptation. She opened the drawer in which she thought she'd find our tableware (and indeed she did), took out a fork, and pitched it into a meatball, which she promptly put into her mouth. Oh, the look old Lina gave her! Noretta, who had seen it, thought it meant

---

[1] Nora Baldi, a friend of Saba and his wife and the author of *Il Paradiso di Saba* (Mondadori, 1958), a memoir of Saba and his world.

that Lina was upset because there wouldn't be enough left for me. But your mother knew very well that I ate only one, or at the most two, never more—the others would just disappear, I don't know how or where. The reason for the dirty look was completely different. My "good and wonderful," my "earthy" Lina would give anything to anyone who asked for it in a nice way, even—as they say—the shirt off her back. But she couldn't bear people, particularly women, who, when they were on her territory, took things that were hers or that she considered hers, without her having first offered them.

Not long after this, however, Noretta and your mother became really close friends. Then Noretta received an "official" invitation to a lunch that consisted exclusively of those meatballs, washed down with two or more bottles of Chianti (Noretta is a good drinker). And it was precisely halfway through this meal that I committed the rash act of interrupting something Lina was saying. I don't remember whether it was to correct what she'd said or just to add something of my own. "Oh, shuddup, you moron," was your mother's unexpected reaction on this occasion. Somewhat embarrassed, I turned to look at Noretta. And to my great, to my joyful, surprise, I saw her large, cold huntress eyes filling with tears she didn't even try to hide. She had understood. Understood, I swear, the depth of emotion, intimacy, and symbiosis that lay behind those few colloquial words your mother had blurted out. And when, a few days before she died, your poor mother committed me to Noretta's care with an unforgettable look, this is what Noretta said: "If you put your *Canzoniere* and everything else you ever wrote on one side of a balance, and on the other you put the love, affection, understanding, tolerance, mercy, and charity that Lina bestowed on you for fifty years (young or old, you could never have been an easy man to live with), there's no doubt about it, the scale would be perfectly balanced."

The second invitation (this time not for lunch, but for dinner) was, as I said before, much more exotic. Our guest was (in addition to Noretta, who had by then become almost one of the family), Count Giacomo Leopardi.[2] I'm not about to tell you how we managed to locate him and

---

[2]Major Italian poet and patriot. Born 1798 in Recanati. Died 1837 in Naples. Known for his pessimism and tragic view of life.

to send him the invitation. Was it reality? A dream?[3] You'll decide that yourself in the end. However, I'll say this again—though your mother found ways other than through literature to express herself, she had loved Leopardi's poetry from her earliest girlhood. The dinner was set for the fifth of June, 1952, at six in the evening (it had to do with the Count's schedule). Our first problems arose in regard to planning the menu. We all knew that in addition to his other complaints and ailments, the poet had a particularly weak stomach and intestinal tract. But after long and interminable consultations among the three of us, and employing a process of elimination (it goes without saying that meatballs, with or without tomato sauce, was among the first dishes to fall by the wayside), we came up with the following menu: a substantial (but not too heavy) broth from which the fat would be completely removed; fish—we hoped to find something really special in the market; and a light, iced dessert. The soup would be served separately, in such a way that our guest could choose to eat it plain or add some spoonfuls of rice to it. Then your mother made the perceptive observation that just because we thought fish was a good idea, it didn't mean our guest would like it. Therefore, just in case, she would prepare a chicken leg and a wing. None of us knew or remembered hearing anything about whether Leopardi's doctors permitted their famous patient to have coffee. However, if he could have it, it would be an easy matter to prepare it at the last minute. As for the frozen dessert, Noretta offered to order it from the best, or at least the most popular, confectioner in Trieste. The only problem left was how to serve at table. We, your poor mother and I, didn't have a regular maid, only a woman who worked by the hour, and even she came just often enough for us to get by. Then I had a brilliant idea. I telephoned your cousin—good, kind, motherly, warmhearted Paoletta. I told her quickly what the story was and asked if

---

[3]According to Nora Baldi in *Il Paradiso di Saba,* the original manuscript did not include these two questions. Instead it read: ". . . and this time too, it was a miracle of love (but then aren't there others?)." The questions "Was it reality? A dream?" were suggested by Carlo Levi for "journalistic reasons," which infuriated Saba. Levi believed that if the piece were too difficult it would not be published. Though Saba finally gave in, he insisted that the original text be used if the story were ever reprinted. In fact, however, the 1964 edition of Saba's *Prose* preserved Levi's suggestions.

she would accept the responsibility on this extraordinary occasion of becoming our maid. She agreed.

On the morning of the fifth, Noretta drove me to the fish market in her car. Even here, my fortune took a good turn. As soon as I walked in, I noticed wonderfully large and fresh looking mullets (a fish not often seen in these parts) on one of the front counters. I chose five of the best looking and had them weighed up. It's true they cost an arm and a leg, but for such an occasion, for such a guest . . . Your mother cooked them on the grill and when they were done poured a little pure olive oil over them. At four-thirty in the afternoon, the impatiently awaited dessert arrived and was promptly put into the refrigerator. Paoletta arrived at about the same time, all smiles and looking pleased with herself in the unaccustomed maid's outfit. (She said she'd borrowed it from her own maid, but I strongly suspected she'd had it made by a fashionable dressmaker). As our usual greetings—our hugs and kisses—were rushed, she immediately asked me, "What's going on, Uncle?" But I told her to keep quiet please, promising I'd explain everything later. The truth is that I, that we, were getting more anxious by the minute. Would the guest we'd waited for and hoped for so long really come? Yes? No? But punctuality is the grace of royalty. And lo! precisely at six, a strange equipage appeared outside our window and pulled up at the front door of the house. It was a coach bearing a coat of arms, drawn by two horses, with a powdered, liveried servant on the front box and another behind. I recognized the coach immediately as the one Her Ladyship, his mother, the Marchese Antici, used regularly to get from the Leopardi mansion to the small nearby church, which was, and still is, situated in the same quiet square. Several minutes later our guest, having been welcomed respectfully at the door by the servant Paoletta, entered. On seeing him we were somewhat surprised. The deformity that caused him so much suffering had almost completely disappeared. Just a trace of it remained and even that was barely visible. He was wearing a gray traveling suit of quite casual cut. His face was the same as always. A smile full of melancholy and sweetness played on his lips. His eyes showed great kindness and, at the same time, an unbearable fatigue, as if he were too strong to die and too weak to live on.

When he was settled in the chair your mother offered him, Paoletta poured him a first ladle of soup. The poet motioned with his hand (a very beautiful hand) to tell her it was enough. However, it pleased him to add a little rice. (Oh, your mother's foresight!) When the time came to serve the fish, Paoletta was the first to notice the change that came over the poet's face, and she offered to skin and debone it for him, something she did immediately with consummate skill and speed. (The smile with which the author of *Silvia* thanked her, the look the count bestowed upon the servant, were almost the high point of the meal.)

But we three were all shy. Each of us had barely enough nerve to address a word to him. So the conversation, as inevitably happens under such circumstances, was about the weather—about how the various seasons bring different discomforts and pleasures (at the word "pleasures" our guest's face darkened—for a moment it even appeared hostile). However, he brightened a bit when he saw the frozen dessert. Paoletta (as I had asked her to in advance) served him a more than adequate portion. Nevertheless the poet asked, almost pleaded, for a second helping. That left only the coffee. Without referring either to illnesses or to doctors, your mother asked him if he would like a small cupful. When he said yes, she decided to make it herself, and left the room. I was dying to read one of his *Idylls* out loud to him while we waited, in the hope that he would praise my interpretation. But it was easy to see that this wasn't going to happen. I decided then that at least I could clear up something I was uncertain about. To write "roses and violets" to describe the flowers that the little maiden had in her hand when she returned from the countryside had seemed to me and to others affected and vague, a small imperfection in a heavenly poem. However . . . had the young maiden really picked those flowers—had the poet really seen them in her hand? With all due deference, I explained my doubts to the author of *Sabbath in the Village*, adding that I had even asked a number of horticulturists whether roses and violets could (without having to be imported or raised in hothouses) blossom at the same time in our countryside. No one, I told him, could give me a precise answer. One connoisseur to whom I explained the reason for my interest answered, "Here, where we are, no. But if it's possible anyplace, it would be at Recanati."

At that moment your mother came in carrying the tray and the coffeepot. And just as miraculously as he had appeared, the poet was gone. We all dashed to the landing of the staircase. No one was there, except the people who were usually in the house. The same thing out the window—just the usual children playing ball, automobiles, trucks as high as houses, motor-cycles and Lambrettas, making the exact opposite of "joyful noise." There was no trace of the poet or his strange equipage. Your mother, to whom I'd briefly mentioned the question I'd asked him, immediately accused me of causing his disappearance. I answered her by saying that if he had arrived here in a certain way, he no doubt had to depart in the same way. Besides, this was hardly the time for faultfinding, as though the matter had been a mere auto accident.

After a long and distressing silence, Noretta, the calmest of us, at least in appearance, spoke the only words that could be said at that awkward moment. French on her mother's side and nurtured by French culture, she brushed the palms of her hands lightly together and drew the moral of this tale (in which she, your mother, and I had participated with so much love) with a line in French that I am afraid I didn't hear well and am therefore repeating imperfectly. "Tout s'est évanoui comme un rêve qu'on a . . ."[4]

Your father

---

[4]"Everything has vanished as if in a dream . . ."

Portrait of Curzio Malaparte

DEAR LINUCCIA,

Before saying anything to you about an unusual individual (representative, however, of our era) whom I am not sure you knew, and before describing "the man" Malaparte, whose acquaintance I made because of the dreary vicissitudes of mankind's insanity, I want to tell you an anecdote about him, though I cannot warrant its authenticity. They say that in the days when Mussolini still wore white gaiters, he met Malaparte in the halls of some ministry and asked, "Why, von Suckert, did you change your name to Malaparte?"

"Because," the latter is said to have replied instantly, "I will lose at Austerlitz and win at Waterloo."[1]

During the era Montale described as "shameful in our history," I found myself not only in a dreadful situation, but an awkward one as well. After my unhappy Parisian experiment[2] I decided that "coûte que coûte," I would return to Italy, which in my heart, as well as legally, was my homeland. Back in "mother" Rome, I immediately went to see my friend Falqui. Racially mixed as I am, I had nothing in the way of papers or anything else that might work in my favor, not even money for bribes. Falqui was pleased to see me again. He told me that the person who could be most helpful in my case was Malaparte. When I said I didn't know him, Falqui immediately rushed to the phone and explained my situation to him as quickly and as well as one could on the telephone in those days. An appointment was set up for the next morning. The man who greeted me was still very young, positively boyish looking. He was, for the most part, handsome. Only the shape of his forehead left me a little uncertain. I recall there was an extremely beautiful yellow German Shepherd lying at his feet, which had been with him during his confinement[3] and which he petted from time to time. Already informed about my situation, he told me that the only way things might perhaps work out for me would be if I were to accept baptism. (At that time there were many priests who, for

---

[1] Napoleon *Buona*parte, of course, was victorious at Austerlitz and defeated at Waterloo.

[2] Saba had fled to Paris in the summer of 1938 to escape Italy's racial laws, but remained there only until early 1939 when this episode took place.

[3] Malaparte had been sent into confinement in the early days of fascism.

a modest offering to the poor or simply out of Christian charity, would baptize people retroactively.) I told him frankly I couldn't do that, not because of any commitment to my mother's Judaism, but because the performance of a religious act as a response to external violence seemed to me to be sacrilegious.

At first Curzio Malaparte looked at me the way an adult looks at a child who knows nothing about life. Then he listened to me with an intensity that seemed excessive. After that we spoke about other things. He showed me some photos of himself sunbathing and swimming when he was in confinement, in which the police who were "guarding" him seemed really to be servants waiting on him. In the discussion that followed, I admired not only his intelligence but also his prodigious memory for people, things, and events. He told me that they were the result of the wonderful education he'd had at the Cicognini School in Prato. Immediately, two ideas occurred to me. First, that Curzio was proud of having been educated in that school because it's where Gabriele D'Annunzio "watched over by sad schoolmasters" had also been educated, and that he, Malaparte, a little too zealous for fame, the greatest, quickest, and widest possible (oh, fame!), saw in that concurrence a good omen for his career as a writer. The second idea is more important and of greater general interest. A good memory is not in the least the result of education, but of courage. In fact, it takes a great deal of courage (a commodity Curzio had to spare), once having passed childhood, to recall the past. But he didn't accept my interpretation, which he called (though it wasn't) Freudian. However, he then told me why he, half German, had enlisted at the age of fifteen (or perhaps he was sixteen) during the First World War and about his father, who had accompanied him to the station carrying his rifle.

After that we maintained a brief correspondence. He was publishing a good and courageous (for that era) review called *Prospettive* (Prospectives). He asked me to write for it using my own name. I sent him several poems (just a few because I was writing few then), which he duly published and paid for. I saw him next in Naples, at the home of a mutual friend where I least expected to see him. He seemed pleased to see me. But what surprised me was that he spent the entire afternoon "preaching" to my friend, who, it seems, was overly generous to friends and acquaintances and (as often happens in such cases) somewhat tightfisted with his wife.

Afterward he invited us to have dinner with him at an unpretentious little tavern, where he changed the subject and made inflammatory remarks about the current regime, the likes of which I had never heard from even the most ardent antifascist. Disloyalty?[4] It's hard to know. But even so, it led the way to another small "revelation." So-called disloyalty isn't, as is generally believed, common. Just the opposite. We poor human beings dissemble, it's true, but intermittently, or because we're compelled to, little by little, by "harsh necessity" (Homer), or by "force of circumstances" (Napoleon), or in self-defense. But to live a life, I'm speaking of an entire life, thinking one thing and writing something else (and constantly juggling all of that) requires—beyond an extraordinary, almost stupefying intelligence—consistency, self-discipline, and courage of the same degree, if not higher. (I'd even add considerable "moral fiber" in terms of concentrating solely on one's own interests.) Perhaps this was in part Curzio Malaparte's "genius," his "trump card."[5] I repeat, I don't know. And anyway, it's not in my nature to make judgments.

When he spent a few days in Trieste and stayed at the city's most luxurious hotel (where he had taken an entire apartment, although, as we'll see, he was essentially modest and compassionate), he came to visit me. But the atmosphere in my poor house was sad and gray. What's more, he was upsetting me by insisting that I write an article for *Prospettive* directed against Trieste's merchants, whom he found (I'm not sure why) particularly repellent. (A fine "prospective" the article would have been for me, and I certainly didn't feel like writing it!) But suddenly, there was Curzio Malaparte looking at your middle-aged mother, who had not been listening to him, clearly absorbed in her own sad thoughts. He interrupted the discussion, approached her as a knight would his lady, and made her dance with him willy nilly around the dinner table. ("Malaparte's Dance" would have been the name of this memory-story, but at the last moment it seemed irreverent to me, inasmuch as he is dead.) Tired and exhausted as your poor mother was, she was touched and smiled her thanks, then—how happily she did it—invited her "knight" for dinner.

---

[4]The word Saba uses is "malafede," a play on Malaparte's name.
[5]The Italian, "buona carte," is yet another play on Malaparte's name.

He accepted, saying, however, that he would have to leave first but would be back in an hour or two. We waited one, two, three hours for him, and when he didn't show up, your mother and I, alone and despondent, nibbled at food that had in the meantime turned cold.

Recuperating many years later in a Roman clinic, I asked him to come visit me. Basically, I liked him, and then I've never been an ingrate. But there was something else on my mind which concerned him and which I wanted to say to him. He came with Falqui. "Look, Curzio," I told him, "you know how to write and to write well." He tried to interrupt me, bringing up that Cicognini di Prato school again, but I didn't let him. This time I was "preaching." "Your books," I told him, "are fine. The only thing that spoils them a little is that they give one the feeling (not always, but often) that they were written to shock the reader and attract even more attention. You were good at that, really good. But there's something else in you, Curzio, that I know is there, a hidden vein of humility and kindness. My wish for you, when you are old, tired, and fed up with fame, is that God will inspire you to use the talent He gave you to write a book to be published only after your death (no fame, therefore, in this world)—an honest book in which you tell the truth, the entire truth, at least as you see it, about the people, facts, and events you've known or experienced in your very full life. I think a great book could come of it."

He heard me out for nearly an hour. Then he said that there was someone downstairs in his car whom he didn't want to keep waiting any longer. He asked me and Falqui to join him and that person at a bar for coffee. I dressed quickly, expecting to find at least a princess down there. Instead, huddled in the corner of an extraordinarily long and luxurious car parked at the clinic door was a pathetic-looking little girl dressed, if you can call it that, in tatters, upon whom Malaparte immediately heaped blandishments and kindnesses, and who, later in the bar, blushed like a schoolgirl when she accepted the small box of caramels I gave her. I knew that even in his friendships, Curzio had this vein of humility, of which I've spoken before, together with a deep, unacknowledged need to cast off the superstructure, the entire superstructure with which, perhaps, he had armored himself to ward off the only kind of fear he could feel. And unless she was a princess in disguise, that little girl confirmed to me, more than ever, my analysis.

I will add, inasmuch as you are elsewhere, far away and remote, as Mme. de Sagan was from Mme. de Sévigné, what Noretta[6] said to me when I read her this recollection for the first time. "You were born innocent and you will die innocent." Maybe.

Nevertheless, though I'm not what one would call a believer, I asked a Jesuit priest here to say a mass for the soul of my friend Curzio Malaparte, who though so totally my opposite, helped me or tried to help me when I was in trouble.

Your father

---

[6]See note on page 144.

From Three Fragments

A Conscript's Dream

"I will tell unbelievable things and true"
Dante, *Inferno*

ONE MORNING AT THE END OF THIS PAST MARCH (1907), I had a strange dream. I found myself on a wide road between a gray, silent sea and a chain of sun-bathed hills lined with plants and red and yellow cottages that looked like suburban houses. I think that road was probably a variant of the road in Trieste that leads from the village of Barcola to the Miramar Castle, not just because of its topographical resemblance, but because of the feeling it gave me—a troubled feeling like that I had as a child whenever I walked along it. The feeling was a mixture of melancholy (a melancholy that often assailed me when I had to be away from the city for an unusually long time—as if I'd never again be able to find my way back to it, to my house, to the security of my good mother, to the pantry full of anticipated delicacies), and of a desire to see all the great new things, all the wondrous places I was sure existed beyond that row of hills, visible from my window, and through which I wandered in imagination. It was a feeling, in short, that I had completely forgotten after such a long span of years, and that now delighted me again in this dream on a spring morning. I was all alone on that road until, turning my head suddenly at the sound of my name, I saw an old man nearby. He was leaning on a thick stick and staring at me with eyes that looked like mine. I didn't recognize his face, but it seemed clear to me that I had seen him before—where or when I couldn't say. While I struggled vainly to recognize this person who had called my name and who had eyes like mine, I was overcome with a sick feeling—the foreboding that accompanies a desperate desire that one knows that one cannot, or dares not, fulfill. That old man, in telling me his great sorrows, in pleading for release from them through the compassion they would undoubtedly evoke in me, would cause me to suffer. It's the feeling you get when, because it's no longer possible, or for some other reason, you've made a firm decision to stop giving money to a beggar, and then see him coming toward you expecting his usual sum. My discomfort grew and became a virtual terror until—after what seemed an eternity—the old man opened his mouth to speak. Immediately I began to run. And just as quickly as my foreboding had turned into terror, my running became a breathless flight and the wide road between the hills and the sea became a slippery path, while the old man, still repeating my name in his cracking voice, kept following me and hitting the ground with his stick, which, like a giant's crutch, gave off a fearful sound. At the same time that I was terrified, I was also tormented by remorse because, young and strong, I had all the advantage over a sick old man. It was too easy to outrun a lame pursuer. And little by little that remorse overcame me, so much so that I stopped running and slowly, fearfully turned my head toward the old man, who in order to reach me had multiplied his efforts and his laments, and was shaking his now apparently unnecessary stick in the leaden air. All at once, staring into those eyes getting ever closer to me, I saw something indefinably evil, something that seemed to say, "See how I, the weaker of us two, have defeated you? And you will come and do everything that I, in my pleading voice, will demand of you. And then you will repent and curse your weakness. But it will be late. Too late."

Portrait of Adele

DEAR LINUCCIA,

When your mother was not much more than a child, she and her family lived for some time in Spalato. Spalato was an enchanting town. I saw it for the first time when I was about nineteen. Today it's called Split; and here you must permit me a small aside. You know that your father loves Italy too much to be what's called a nationalist. It is enough for him to be a national. But the name Split, by which that lauded city has been known since the end of the First World War, never ceases to remind me of three lines of poetry by Gabriele D'Annunzio, "For the Sailors Who Died in China." They are:

> At Sebenico, Spalato and Gravosa
> on the Latin coast
> where San Marco tied his galley

Forgive me—it's just a literary issue—but rightly or wrongly, the name Spalato affects me much more than Split.

To return to your mother and to begin this portrait of your aunt Adele with your mother's recollection (even in death that woman still gives me gifts), I will tell you that the greatest pleasure her family could give your mother was to permit her to take her little sister, who was nearly three years old, out for a walk, reminding her (unnecessarily) to hold her tightly by the hand. She would let the baby lead the way—go everywhere she wanted, except the one place little Adele would have liked best, a pastry shop. She didn't have the few pennies a pastry cost in those days. Perhaps your mother, who as I said was not much more than a child herself, liked them too. But it would have been enough for her, even more pleasing, to delight the little sister whose hand she was holding. With what devotion she watched over her. Unfortunately, your mother had two handicaps for the Spalato of that era. She, who from the time I met her "occupied little space in this world," looked older than she was and was already "well-developed." This last quality seemed to be especially attractive to Dalmatian men, who—unwelcomely—followed her through the streets. (You have to understand that during the distant era I'm talking about, when a Dalmatian man mentioned his wife, he almost always preceded it with "respectfully speaking." Sometimes he would even spit on the ground, even though his wife were following him at the prescribed six paces.) Finally, one day, such a man (I think, though I'm not sure, that he was a stationer), holding an enormous, elegantly dressed doll, stopped the two girls. He raised his hat to a respectful, if not higher, level and asked your mother's permission to give the doll to the little girl, saying, and perhaps it was true, that he had never seen a more beautiful child. You can imagine your aunt Adele's reaction, when wide-eyed, as if she had just caught a glimpse of heaven, she put her hand out to grasp that miraculous item, and instead saw your mother pull away from the giver and the gift, whose significance she had only too well understood. A life (her own) for a doll. Adele screamed, cried, shouted, refused to budge, looked back in vain for the man to return, and with her free hand hit your mother, who at that moment must have seemed a cruel tyrant, an incomprehensible monster to her. Nothing worked. Your mother cut short the walk and brought her screaming little sister home, where everyone agreed she had done the right thing. Little Adele, however, hardly ate her supper, asked to go right to bed, and probably still crying, fell asleep quickly.

Who knows, who can ever know how it affected all the rest of her life, that a gift which seemed to have dropped from heaven was, for totally incomprehensible reasons, forbidden to her in her needy childhood. And if she dreamed that night, what dreams did three-year-old Adele have? The following day she seemed to have forgotten the doll and the incident, which means, at least to me, that they weren't really forgotten (one never forgets anything), but had simply fallen into the (almost) unfathomable depths of the unconscious.

The first time I saw Adele (your mother had told me about the doll episode many years after it occurred) was at dinner at her family's house. She came home cranky and late, and paid absolutely no attention to me, even though she knew that I wanted to marry her sister. I don't think she even listened for my name, but sat down at the table where her dinner, a salad and a dish of stew that had been kept warm, were still waiting. She wanted to eat the salad first, but on tasting it, her eyes shot sparks. "This salad is spoiled," she said, pushing her plate across the table. Everyone (especially your grandmother) protested, but it made no difference. She ate the stew quickly, as if unaware that in my honor it was hare stew, then, without a glance or a word for anyone, went immediately into her room. (All of them in that house were hotheads and, except for poverty, and sometimes style, aristocrats.) That was my first encounter with her.

In my second, I saw her nude. I inadvertently opened the door into the room where she, who with good reason was called "the most beautiful girl in Trieste," was taking her daily bath in a washtub. I saw not Venus of the furtive eyes but Diana beloved of Hippolytus, or better still, Minerva. In all my life I have rarely seen anything so perfect, chaste, and pure.

From Shortcuts and Very Short Stories

1934–1948

Selections from the First Shortcuts

I

WRITING SHORTCUTS. They are full of parentheses, of "between the hyphens," "between the commas," of words underlined in the manuscript which have to be printed in italics, of capitalized words, of "three dots," of exclamation points and question marks. May the typesetter first, then the reader, forgive me. I can't say anymore without shortening things, and there was no other way I could do it.

2

SHORTCUTS—says the dictionary—are the shortest way to get from one place to another. They can be difficult at times, really goat trails, and they make you yearn for long, flat, paved straightaways.

3

LAST STRAW. In a house where one person hangs himself, where others kill each other, where some are prostitutes, and some are dying painfully of hunger, where still others are destined for jail or the madhouse, a door opens, and you can see an old woman playing the spinet. Playing it very well.

4

HISTORY OF ITALY. Have you ever asked yourself why Italy, in all its history—from Rome to the present day—has never had even one true revolution? The answer—a key that opens many doors—lies perhaps in a few lines of its history.

Italians are not patricides. They are fratricides. Romolo and Remus, Ferrucio and Maramaldo, Mussolini and the socialists, Badoglio and Graziani... "We will struggle, brother against brother," the latter declared in one of his manifestos. (Favored, though not necessitated, by circumstance, it was a cry from the heart, the cry of one who—once he saw it clearly—finally gave vent to his feelings.) Italians (I believe) are the only people, whose history (and legends) are based on fratricide. And it is only with patricide (killing the old) that one can start a revolution.

Italians want to devote themselves to their fathers and to receive from them, in exchange, permission to kill their brothers.

5

AFTER NAPOLEON each of us is a little better, if only because Napoleon once lived. After Maidaneck . . .[1]

6

NAPOLEON was a man. Like all men—(a few) criminals excluded—he *also* had a sense of guilt. And one has the impression that at the end of his life it dominated him. He was not tormented by the thought of the men who had been killed in his wars, but by remorse—which he tried as hard as he could to distance from his conscience—for having abandoned, for having *had* to abandon, "his good (unfaithful) Josephine." And when he came back from Russia, he suffered for a long time, calling her name in an empty Malmaison.

Like a child who, having wronged his mother, runs away from home— each time to travel a little farther away. He returns one evening, down-hearted and tired, and discovers that his mother can no longer—even if she so wished—forgive him. She is dead. Then he weeps.

This isn't a poetic invention. It is a truth; a small, simple, human truth (even Napoleon was simple), which goes further than you may think to explain the absurd Russian campaign. It explains the fatal internal flaw

---

[1] *Saba's note:* Several of the few readers of this difficult book have asked me what or who Maidaneck was. Maidaneck was a small German concentration camp: the first discovered by the Allied forces. At the time, newspapers and magazines published photos of the wretched survivors. Buchenwald, Auschwitz, etc. were still unknown.

from which it grew, and the reason (I wouldn't want to alarm anyone by calling it self-punishing) for which it was conceived.

7

FOR THOSE who still believe that Adolf Hitler (the man who could not love) had *at least* loved Germany, I will here describe what his dream *really* was.

To reduce Germany to a pile of rubble; and, amid clouds of lethal gas, to rebuke the German people for having—through the fault of the Jews—betrayed him, whereupon HE rises into Heaven in a kind of apotheosis, surrounded by the flower of his youngest and most faithful ss.

He dreamed this dream so profoundly (believing—oh, in all good faith!—that he would dream another such) that one can say he may have won—at least in part—HIS war.

9

A SMALL BLACK BOY enters a Soviet school for the first time. In every other country—he complains—the children used to persecute him. No one wanted to play with him because of the color of his skin. Now (says the very short story, perhaps an illustrated tale) his new friends gather around him, console him, caress him, offer him sweets. Finally, they teach him to say Lenin's name. And after that, they set him in front of a mirror. He was white.

"What foolishness! We've read such tales, too many of them in state-issued books for our children." That isn't true. Fascism couldn't invent a happy fable. Its fables were dismal, like its ditchdiggers' uniforms.

10

COCTEAU. After more than ten years, I still remember Cocteau's *Orfeo*. This is how I remember it.

A husband, upset because he hasn't won a poetry prize, is quarreling with his wife. A window shatters. In comes a workman to repair it. The husband doesn't (or pretends not to) notice, though the woman, appalled, does see that the workman is doing his job *without touching the ground*. He's floating in the air. "I'm tired of mysteries," she explodes. "I called for a glazier, not an angel."

14

TO CREATE, just as to understand art, one thing is necessary above all: that somewhere in us our childhood be preserved. But this is something the very process of living tends to destroy. The poet is a child who, having reached adulthood, marvels at the things that happened to him. *But how much of an adult is he?*

Here we touch on one of the differences between insignificant and great poetry. Only where the child and the man coexist in the most extreme form possible, and in the same person, aided as well by other favorable factors, can a miracle be created. Such a miracle is Dante. Dante is a small child continually amazed at what happens to a grown man. They are truly "two in one." See how the small Dante is startled, shouts, is overcome with joy, shakes with anger and with (simulated) fear, exalts, shows off, humbles himself coquettishly, rises toward the stars before the extraordinary events that are created through him, through a bearded Dante in magistrate's robes! And how he enjoys those prizes and those punishments (the punishments more than anything else), those devils and those angels, those "courteous doorkeepers," those living and those dead more alive than the living. What an unbelievable journey! How can one hope for a more brilliant feast, more brilliant light? And opposite him, united with him, Dante; Dante the complete man, husband, father, warrior, political man, unhappy and glorious exile; Dante with all the tremendous passions of his era and of his maturity battling against others and (less) against himself, against those the facts say are always wrong, always more certain of being right, and therefore always *staring in amazement*, bedazzled by hate and love.

If the man prevails too much over the child (Montale suggests as an example of this the venerated name of Goethe), the poet (as poet) leaves us cold. If there is almost only a child, and a stalk with only the barely formed embryo of a man, we have the "boy poet" (Pascoli). We feel dissatisfied with him and a little ashamed.

15

THE FATHER with a son in a difficult situation—let's say, to take an extreme case, in a war—who thinks of him continually as in danger, and who inevitably sees him as dead, doesn't love his son. Or, to be exact, doesn't only love him. Love is not a forecaster of disaster. *Love sees through rose-colored glasses*. And sometimes, of course, it fools us.

17

THE PASSERBY who takes pleasure in telling you that your shoelaces are undone is a useless person. Perhaps you knew it yourself and are looking for an out-of-the-way place to fix them. Or perhaps you are being pursued by the Furies. In the first instance, he is just a nuisance. In the second . . .

18

WHEN ONE GETS to a certain age, it is no longer possible to carry on debates. One can only learn or teach. To learn would still be best. But who can teach an old man? He has to learn by himself, or disappear.

19

I HAVE NOTHING to say to philosophers. And they have nothing to say to me. As they get closer they become fluid; they expand on the universal in order not to be touched at a sensitive spot. All their systems are patch-work, to hide a "rupture in reality."

Poets promise less and provide more.

22

ITALO SVEVO'S BEEFSTEAK. Italo Svevo (who, as everyone who knew him understood, had mythic as well as human ways) was happy to tell (and did so more than once, as old people, who like to repeat themselves, do) that he had never enjoyed eating a steak as he did toward the end of the First World War, when he was (or thought himself to be) the only person in the city able to have one.

He wasn't—oh, no!—a devil among so many angels. He was merely an artist, and as one he accepted everything in nature, within himself and without. He was merely admitting what other men (good and pure men) were either unaware of feeling, or what they hid behind—a more or less conspicuous veil of hypocritical tears.

But without his realizing it, in the story of his beefsteak he touched on the real problem of world economics and revealed the genesis of its disasters. That Brazil (to take the most common example) lines its streets with coffee beans so that countries that don't produce them can't buy them cheaply is not fundamentally an economic issue, but a psychological one. It is only secondarily (because man is what he is) that it becomes a concern of economists. Svevo's beefsteak teaches us that man is still too much of a child to enjoy a good thing without placing some emphasis on the fact that others don't have it, and that the particular good is his privilege (as the only, or the preferred, child). If this weren't so, what with all the means of production and transportation available today, there would not be any poverty or hunger in the world. It would take so little to find a way to arrange this. But I know that that "little" is a mere illusion, just a way of speaking, and that before man learns to read, to spell out a syllable more in *that* direction, the heavens will have to open and strike him. And more than once.

23

THOSE PEOPLE, and there are many of them, who even today believe that wars break out for economic reasons, are saying the same thing as those who say the Germans gassed six and a half million Jews in order to make fertilizer out of them. They used gas for other reasons (for some obscure reactions having to do with physics). But once murdered, they made use—and why not?—of the corpses to the advantage of the (new) chosen people.

Wars are fought because man is an aggressive animal, perhaps the most aggressive in creation. He feels that if he does not express his aggression toward others, it will turn in against himself. And that if he doesn't attack others, he will, sooner or later, end up attacking himself. And that would cause him more suffering than going to war. Thus (sublimation being a long and difficult path, open to only a few) he prefers to be killed killing, than to kill himself in the silence of his own room.

This is the "religious" origin (he would have done better to have said "instinctive") that old Moltke ascribed to war. Economic causes "coexist." They are for the most part—at least today—pretexts offered to the instinct for death.

Rome
February 1945

28

WAGNERIANS are suspect not because they love Wagner but because they love *only* Wagner.

30

A YOUNG COMMUNIST retorted to my—much humiliated!—individualism, "What would you be, if there were nobody else around?"

They were the most profound words I'd heard in years. Their simple human reality saved my old legs a lot of walking. Once again I can take the tram, fight my way onto the running board, and tolerate the crowds.

31

I AM NOT by nature a revolutionary. I am a conservative of the rarest kind. I understand—I've always understood—that one has to renounce a great deal in order to conserve an essence.

A pure conservative doesn't think like that. Or better still, he doesn't think at all. He is just constipated.

32

PATRIOTISM, nationalism, and racism rank as do health, neurosis, and insanity.

33

NATIONALISM exemplifies, as does neurosis, the other side of a coin, when the exaggeration of a feeling, such as love of one's country, which is so natural to man, becomes the source of its negation.

Italian nationalists derived their theories from the French. They wanted to be French. But the France of French nationalists wasn't the country of their own era, it was another France, long dead, France around Louis XIV's time.

Nationalists are bad sons. They want to change their mothers. Don't love their God-given ones enough.

35

THE TWENTIETH CENTURY seems to have only one desire: to get to the twenty-first as quickly as possible.

37

HERMETICISM. Crossword puzzles. More—in Montale—in the poetry of Montale. It owed its success (at least at the beginning) to crossword puzzles.

38

THE TYPEWRITER—used by poets before their words see print—has been a good influence on them and on poetry, *noxious to the superfluous*. It was lovely to type out a war poem by Ungaretti. But a long, sentimental poem!

39

WHEN I WAS a guardian of the noble dead (an antiquarian book dealer), Carletto (my good employee) asked permission to take time off to visit a dear sister in Sicily. The needs of the small business (which only we two looked after) made it impossible for me to grant him this intensely desired wish at that particular time, and I had to say no.

"What strange dreams you can have sometimes, signor Saba. Imagine, last night I dreamed that I landed on an island with a group of men about my own age and the old captain of the ship. All of us together stoned him to death. But walking away, I felt sort of remorseful, so I turned around. And the old man was still alive. I was so relieved, Signor Saba! I was really happy when I woke up!"

I didn't try to explain this easy dream to Carletto, but I did give him the permission he wanted. A little, in gratitude, for having brought me back to life.

40

CARLETTO. When a pile of books was about to fall, he would shout at them to stay still. He wouldn't have accepted my interpretation of his dream (he'd have shrugged his shoulders and mumbled to himself). But he believed in magic.

41

BRITISH SOLDIER. In a bar in the heart of Florence, a very young British soldier—he was almost a boy—was trying to charm the barkeeper into serving him beer. But the barkeeper, who was prohibited by law from serving alcohol to Allied troops, though uncomfortable, refused him. However, as soon as I asked for it, he gave me a glass of wine, which the soldier eyed enviously. How happy he would have been to have it! And even while drinking, how happy I'd have been to give it to him. He showed his conflicting feelings saying "Salute!" right in my face, though in a piteous voice. Then he delicately flicked a grain of dust from the lapel of my overcoat. After that he walked out onto the crowded street, where, to prove to himself that he'd already had enough drink and that he was feeling happy, he began, under his breath, and in the thin voice of a chastened child, to sing an army ditty.

43

TUBERCULOSIS, CANCER, FASCISM. Every epoch has its physical illness, to which there is a corresponding one (and probably the same one) in the moral sphere. The nineteenth century had tuberculosis and mawkish sentimentality. The twentieth has cancer and fascism. The entire course of fascism—the way it manifests its true nature when it is already too late for an effective surgical intervention; the impossibility of killing it without also killing the victim in which it has taken root; its tendency to reproduce in places distant from its original site; the desperate sufferings it causes in those it strikes; the profound destruction that shows up on postmortem examination of the bodies (or countries) over which it had total reign—everything in its course, I say, has a surprising similarity to that of cancer. But there is another resemblance as well.

There is no one today who doesn't know that tuberculosis is very often one of the ways young people choose to commit suicide. I'll hazard the hypothesis that cancer (an illness of old people) has its psychic roots in a mistaken attempt by the organism to rejuvenate itself. The formation of a neoplasm could indicate the desire to create a new organ, that is, a new stomach. (I presented this hypothesis to several intelligent physicians, who took it quite seriously.) Well, what was the fundamental reason for the acceptance of fascism in Italy—and everywhere else—if not a mistaken attempt by the bourgeoisie to create a new life for themselves, to rejuvenate themselves? It was too late when they discovered their error, and by then, there was no longer any remedy. The good, the providential thing, which had represented itself as the bearer of a "new order," brought them instead inhuman sufferings, and after varying lengths of time, death.

The "Roman Empire" (of the twentieth century!), unfortunately for us, had the genesis, character, and consequences of a cancer.

44

DOCTORS. Almost the only difference between a good doctor and a bad one is this: that the former loves a cure and the latter loves illness. The bad doctor *does not want* to completely cure a sick person but merely to relieve the symptoms that are causing him to suffer. Thus, the patient, grateful for relief, will come back.

(This reasoning is—of course—not conscious. Or barely . . .)

45

NO YOUTH can call himself well bred (by which I mean of a highly refined sensitivity) who in the presence of a man of genius (or one so reputed) feels himself anything but a hatchling in an eagle's clutches. But perhaps this is a youthful recollection.

46

VERDI. An artist almost too lustful to be an artist. I didn't like Verdi very much when I was young. "All his characters," I would say, "sing divinely with alcohol on their breath." But "divinely" is a word I added later.

One evening, when I was confined to army barracks and alone in an enormous white dormitory, another soldier (Gobbetti was his name—he came from Lombardy, in fact, from Milan) suddenly walked in singing "Bella figlia dell'amore." And all of Italy, with its seas, mountains, and cities, filled my heart with heavenly radiance.

48

THE SHARP, shrill cries of babies in their cradles, or being pushed in carriages to take the sun by their loving mothers, recall at very close quarters the "Tomorrow the world!" of Adolf Hitler.

49

DEAR READER, don't let the sometimes paradoxical, sometimes even playful (?) appearance of (some) of these shortcuts fool you. They were created out of more than ten years of experience of life, art, and sorrow.

They are, more than anything else, in some ways, survivors of Maidaneck.

Rome
March 1945

Selections from the Third Shortcuts

51

CLOCKS. Time is round. It comes back to itself. And clocks, whose purpose it is to tell time, should also be round. They were in fact round from the time they were invented until yesterday.

The recently established practice of giving watches rectangular, triangular, and octagonal shapes is one of the many small indications of the confusions of our days. Of the thousands.

52

GOLD. Mephistopheles knew—yet didn't know—what it meant when he advised the impoverished emperor, who wanted to go to war, to print the first paper money. With this (thoughtfully heeded) advice he facilitated the outbreak of wars. But at the same time, he dealt the harshest blow to avarice, from which he had also drawn much fuel for his fires.

It is easier for man to free himself from a piece of paper than from a round gold piece.

53

THE POET, THE DOG, AND THE HEN. The poet Sandro Penna was very fond of a hen which his mother (perhaps to get its eggs) would let roam throughout the house as if it were a person. But later he acquired a large bitch. And *immediately,* the hen bored him. "Would I love it," he said, "if the dog ate the hen! I even tried handing it to her, but she wouldn't take it. How about that! She turned up her nose at it!"

She turned up her nose because she thought Penna was offering it to her to tempt her, and that if she succumbed to the temptation, he would punish her. In the face of the commandment of our original master—received millenia ago, and now autonomous within us—"THOU SHALT NOT KILL OTHER CREATURES OF MY-YOUR HOUSE"—neither the invitation nor the order of the present master could succeed. If Penna really wants to be rid of an inconvenient friend, he'll have to find another way to do it.

54

DRAMA WITH THREE CHARACTERS (who live in each of us). The Id, from dark, organic, still-unexplored reaches, shouts, "Strike the blow."

"If you do it," the Superego intrudes immediately, "I'll punish you till death, and (who can tell) maybe even after (if I can). But if you don't do it, you're a coward."

And the poor Ego, like Faust, cries out, "Why was I ever born?"

55

MYSTERY NOVELS. They recall the lengthy adventures of wandering knights. In place of knights, however, we have detectives. But (as everything in an era fits together) these detectives (though for different reasons) employ techniques used by psychoanalysts. The clue that solves a case is never where you expect to find it.

56

MYSTERY NOVELS. Every art (every activity) has a particular "climate," in which, over a long period of time, it can attain perfection. Bel canto is Italian, cinematography American, and the detective story British.

This is based on an aspect of law that prohibits the British police from arresting a suspect until they have sufficient evidence to convince a jury of his guilt. In the meantime the killer is free to roam the streets, and continues—to the delight of the "innocent" (?) reader—to commit a series of homicides. This is precisely what happened before our horrified eyes in Europe. Nazism—an enormous mystery novel (I repeat, everything in an era fits together)—had, until the English decided to intervene and induced others to do so, all the time it needed.

57

MYSTERY NOVELS. They are the only contemporary literature that may truly be called popular literature—full of *things* and *facts* and highly diverting incidents (but isn't that the way novels should always be?). And it is also British in this: that there is no other country in the world (I believe) in which the abiding affection of the public for its police agencies, or the civility of the police toward the public, would be believable.

I still remember reading this. A young woman is wandering breathlessly through the streets of London. It is night. An enormous policeman approaches her, taps his helmet, and asks her with some embarrassment, "What's the matter, miss. Is anything wrong?"

58

MYSTERY NOVELS. Just as tales of chivalry gave birth to *Orlando Furioso* and *Don Quixote,* it is possible that some day, a great author will extract from the boundless, raw material of the detective stories a popular work of style.

59

NIETZSCHE, my Nietzsche, my good Nietzsche (not that Nietzsche of others) is so fascinating because he speaks to one's soul and about the soul in the way Carmen spoke to Don José about love. "One never gets tired of that girl!" he told Merimée, just before dying for her. And we never get tired of Nietzsche. Nietzsche wasn't a philosopher. He was the epitome of an almost complete sublimation of Eros.

He was other things too, I know.

60

HEINE. He emerged from the French Revolution (and from elsewhere) as a drummer boy for Napoleon. Like the veteran Legrand (whose stories he heard as a child, and with whom he identified), he believed he was sounding the reveille throughout Europe for forces of liberty. But his *Buch der Lieder*—wrote a French anti-Semite—will be read as long as there are young men to love young women.

61

FREUD. The implacability of honesty, honesty almost to the point of sadism. "Nothing comes of compromising with the truth. It is better—if nothing else will do—to die honestly."

These words, which I am told he spoke, are an *enduring* principle of health. They would have pleased one of his predecessors a great deal: Nietzsche.

62

SENSE OF DIRECTION. My friend Sergio Solmi was a dreadful companion for walking in the city. Whether he couldn't interrupt his train of thought, or whether because of some unfortunate childhood experience, he had no sense of direction, and when you were out with him you would inevitably miss appointments, trams, and trains. In short, *you were sure to get lost.* How many times, visiting him in his bustling Milan, had I complained to him about this fault!

Well, it so happened that he was arrested by the nazifascists (what a word!) and taken to some kind of prison. After a while, he asked if he could use the bathroom. A guard went along with him, but when he came out, the guard (probably tired of waiting) was gone. So Solmi began walking back to his cell by himself. And of course—even here—*he got lost!* Totally without intention, he found himself at the prison gates. No nazifascist ever set eyes on him again.

So now what will I say to him, when I see him and embrace him once more? Will I complain again about his lack of a sense of direction? Or will I tell him that sometimes our defects—like guardian angels—lead us by the hand?

63

WINE, WOMEN, TOBACCO, and other stupefacients destroy a man[1] only if

---

[1]The Italian proverb is: "Bacco, tabacco e venere/riducono l'uomo in cenere," wine, tobacco, and women reduce men to ashes.

he feels guilty about using them—if he struggles with the belief that they are bad for him, and with remorse that he cannot abstain from them. It is a little bit like the story of Svevo's last cigarette. It is also like the not any the less famous story (each of us has heard it many times) of the alcoholic or the drug addict—deplorable examples!—who lives on healthy as an ox into his eighties and nineties, and finally dies as the result of some accident.

Doctors, ordinary people say, "He was made of iron." It's not a question of what he was made of. It's what he was doing. But he was doing it without conflict, and therefore with a clear conscience. It was that clear conscience that enabled him to get rid of the poisons.

64

IN A UNIVERSITY TOWN a while ago, a strange theory had currency among the students (perhaps it still does). Art, all art—including Dante and Petrarch (they actually said Petrarch and Dante), Michelangelo, Leopardi, Mozart, and Beethoven—was a factor of intelligence, nothing but intelligence.

In order for these students, who were not stupid (many of them had or were about to receive degrees in philosophy), to say such an unintelligent thing, the theory had to be of some *use* to them. It's easy to see that it was. If, let's say, a Beethoven adagio (I won't say a Verdi melody, because like them, at their age I didn't like Verdi either) could be produced by felicitous intellectual luck or work; they, the intelligent ones were . . .

With intelligence alone, my dear young friends of Florence, you can do nothing, not even succeed in business, which is the easiest thing in the world to do. There's not much more to a successful firm than an adding machine, operated by a typist, which records and displays the procedures performed.

65

"OH, POOR THINGS!" said fierce Ichino when she understood—and as soon as she read the first words, she did understand—where the above shortcut was leading. Therefore for her sake, for my own, and for love of the truth, I will add (although it isn't relevant) that during the German occupation, those young friends (fanatic as they were about intelligence) behaved admirably. At the risk of their own lives, they helped people whom they neither loved, nor could love, hide and escape, me among them.

68

ARTISTS. Why are artists, even those who have the deepest, most intimate and conscious awareness of their own worth, so inconsolable in the face of failure? "Why isn't it enough for you?" a woman asked one of these inconsolable beings, "why isn't it enough to know what you've done?"

Evidently it is not enough. A work of art is *always* a confession, and like every confession, it requires absolution. Lacking success means being denied absolution. One can only imagine what follows.

69

ROME, I've been told, is like a Negro mother, full of dreadful defects. But I would add that Negro mothers are the most loving—and therefore the best—in the world.

71

SICILIAN SPRING. Bianca—my lovely hostess—was born in Messina. She is all light—with no shadows in which my fatigue can find shelter.

73

PEDAGOGY. In order for teacher and scholar to be perfect for each other, it is necessary that this silent dialogue continuously pass between them: "If only I were still a child like you!" "If only someday, dear teacher, I could be as good as you."

This is the reason women learn so easily. They learn *through love*.

74

HOW MUCH GREATER IS RACINE insofar as he is French. And Leopardi insofar as he is Italian. Is there a great German writer about whom one can say the same?

The great German writers—Goethe, Heine, Nietzsche, as well as others—inveighed against their own country more than any other nation's. Certainly they loved it, but unlike the French and Italians, they didn't want to resemble it.

75

A RACIAL TRIAL. It is such a pleasure to say nice things about what one loves that—although it's not a shortcut and makes no pretense of even making a point—I want to tell how a racial trial unfolded here, in my dear, beloved Italy.

A young officer who had (in 1942) married a Jewish girl was, as a result of the insistant pressure brought to bear by the (sad to say) inevitable spy, expelled from the army and put on trial. The proceedings (after months of fearful anxiety) lasted five minutes and went like this.

The presiding officer (a colonel, I think) asked the accused about his background, and if he felt guilty about having contravened certain laws, etc. etc., in having married such and such a woman who belonged (and here he seemed to pause) to the "Jewish race." After this, and without waiting for a response, the colonel stood up, put his hand on the young man's shoulder, and said, "Don't worry. You didn't do anything wrong. In fact, I'm told that you have a very beautiful wife. So hurry back to her now, and one of these days you'll be recalled and given your new assignment."

In contrast to my friend Giacomo Debenedetti—who writes about this sort of sad happening from his own point of view, and does it very well—I speak and write about it unwillingly. And if, in spite of everything, this very short story demonstrates a point, it is that we Italians *still* are—with exceptions, all the more shameful for being exceptions—among the best people on earth.

76

A COMPELLING RHYME. Ten more years of *fascism, nazism, racism,* and we would have all regressed (literally) to *cannibalism.*

77

FROM HIS BLARING loudspeaker, Doctor Goebbels poisoned the world with his propaganda. Within the limits of my few abilities, I am trying in the columns of *Nuova Europa*[2] to detoxify it with shortcuts.

To each his own.

---

[2]Newspaper in which the *shortcuts* regularly appeared.

Selections from the Fourth Shortcuts and a Very Short Story

78

"PAPA," said one young girl to another of the same age, "is a child with lots of means at his disposal."

79

WOMEN WHO WRITE have, in the past few years, made much praiseworthy progress. Others, there's no doubt, will do so in the future. But if the admirers of their novels, translations, and poetry will pardon me, the works by women that I like best (as I told Gianna Manzini yesterday) are letters and memoirs. And of the last—may the shade of Marcel Proust forgive me—the one to which I return most often (at least in my thoughts) is À La Recherche du Temps Perdu.
   "And Sappho?"
   "Sappho was a swallow and doesn't make a spring."

80

À LA RECHERCHE DU TEMPS PERDU. The most beautiful book ever written by a woman. It engages the reader in endless, charming gossip. Gossip transformed into great poetry.

84

MADNESS—Doctor Weiss explained to me one time—has the same mechanism and serves the same compensatory function as a dream. IT IS A DREAM FROM WHICH ONE DOESN'T AWAKEN.
   A Roman Jewish woman had three sons. One took his own life, another was taken away by the Germans, the third became ill with tuberculosis. A few days before the last one died, the woman began saying that the reason her sons didn't come to see her was that it was impossible for them

to do so. They had all become aides to the king, who was now so devoted to them that he couldn't bear to part with them for even a moment. Her delirium implied many things, even that she—old and impoverished as she was—had married the king (the good father of her infancy, the Prince Charming of her adolescence) and that the latter—in gratitude—had elevated her sons to be his adjutants. It was a fairy tale. The exact opposite of the horrible reality.

The Germans, finding that this miserable woman was a dangerous enemy to the (new) chosen people and a valuable quarry, paid their spy the usual sum in such cases (they say it was five thousand) and took her away too.

Poor, poor humanity!

87

MARIO SPINELLA telephoned me this evening to ask if he could come see me. He had, he said, something to tell me about the shortcuts. I like him (he was wonderful during the clandestine era), and of course, I was expecting praise. I told him to come right over.

He did, in fact, come immediately. What he had to tell me was that neither he nor his friends (young Communists) knew what to make of the shortcuts. They are, he explained, small, felicitous items, born of happiness. (Pehaps what he meant was of the liberation.) He liked Giacomo Debenedetti's work about the Jews and the death camps. Blood and tears came through in that.

Perhaps Spinella was right. Maidaneck cannot be expiated.

92

AN UNPLEASANT CHARACTERISTIC OF ROMANS. In Rome when you walk into a store and ask for something they sell, they treat you (and it's not scheming) with genuine warmth and deep kindness. But if it's your bad luck to ask for something they don't have, they look at you really suspiciously, as though your request was an intentional personal insult.

That's the way it was when, having ordered a soda in a bar that was temporarily out of it, the response I got was one of those dry Neville Chamberlain "no"s, which during the Spanish war were the despair of antifascists and the inspiration for ever more fanciful newspaper headlines.

93

FABLE. If (and luckily, this is impossible) you had absolutely no aggressive instincts and a tiger came roaring at you, you would let yourself be devoured without even understanding what was happening to you.

(Dr. Weiss invented this story to illustrate a point to me.)

94

FACTS preexist. We discover them in living them.

95

POETS. When, during a meal, a critic spoke well to a poet I like of another poet (Montale), the poet tried, and we were just at the pasta, *to poke his eyes out with a fork*. With this (fortunately thwarted) act, the young and slightly drunk Ungaretti demonstrated (1) how much of a poet he was, and (2) how irremediably infantile poets are.

99

TRIESTE. Italy has given us fascism. And that was a horrible thing. Yugoslavia (more precisely the Croats) gave us Pavelic and his Ustashi troops, who were, if possible, even more murderous. They have, it's true, paid dearly with large amounts of blood.

Italian Trieste has given Italo Svevo, Umberto Saba, and several canvases (if they still exist) by the great painter Vittorio Bolaffio. I'm not a nationalist. And I have no interest in throwing oil on the fire, but I know that we are placed, even more than is really necessary, on the side of evil.

But if the things I've mentioned—poetry, paintings, novels—still have any weight, they belong—without counterparts—on *our* side of the scale.

100

SVEVO could write well in German. He preferred writing *badly* in Italian. It was the ultimate homage to the assimilatory charm of the "old" Italian culture. It is a story of love—before the "redemption"—of Trieste for Italy.

101

THE GERMAN GOD (a 1933 portrait). With that mustache under his nose and a grimace on his face, as if he were constantly smelling some bad odor. And he really is. Though it doesn't come—as he thinks it does—from the outside (from Communists, Jews, Poles, and other Slavic peoples, from intellectuals of the right or the left, from the degenerate French and so on, up to and including the entire populated world), but from himself. From inside himself. It's an illness, a nasty illness, and as far as science is concerned, an incurable one. It is called paranoia.

102

IF I HAD to approach that God, I would have done it—physical fear apart—as if I were a doctor approaching the bed of a very sick person.

103

FREUD wouldn't have said anything to him. But—if he had to speak—he would have said (in my opinion): Anti-Semitism . . . They like people. But not *those* people.

104

GOETHE would have told him (I think): Leave the Jews alone. Treated well, they bring prosperity; badly, misfortune.

108

TOTEM AND TABOO. The evening on which it was known—from radio and newspaper announcements—that the executions would take place, there was a restless, festive air in the most crowded sections of Rome. Most of the excitement was centered in the butcher shops, which were very well stocked (it was also just before the first of May). Customers crowded them and seemed more willing than usual to spend money. But as these things go beyond politics, beyond right and wrong, and reason (they follow ancient instinctual patterns), by the following day at the tavern where I usually ate, I could already perceive the first symptoms of remorse. People tried to explain what had happened by twists and hidden turns, in words understandable only to those who might have had some inkling of the language of the unconscious. They said, "It was a good thing to shoot him. In fact they should have done it sooner. It would have been much better *for him* and for us. But there were plenty of others they should have shot with him, even before him [and here followed first and last names of other relatively young people; *brothers* rather than fathers]. But instead they were free. You'll see for how long. *Where'd you get the idea he was guiltier than anyone else?*" etc. etc.

111

IN ROME, a friend of mine, who wishes to remain anonymous, told me, no one (?) works. The city lives—substantially and spiritually—on small intrigues. During the occupation, all those small intrigues had become one enormous plot against the Germans. And when they left, patriotic and personal satisfactions apart, for a long time afterward, my friend (and he swore to me that he was not the only one) felt as depressed as if he'd lost his job.

112

PEOPLE, even the best of them, are not so concerned about having things, as they are about others not having them, or having less.

"Why?" asks the singing voice of small, dark, charming, fierce, little Erna to whom, while we were both seated under the awning of a Triestine tavern, I was telling that "moral tale" you already know, dear reader, the story of "Italo Svevo's Beefsteak."

113

THE MOST BEAUTIFUL LINES IN ITALIAN LITERATURE to me now are: "Trembling, he kissed my mouth"[3] and "They will swindle each other, Your Holiness."[4]

I've known the first one for a long time. I came across the second at the end of the war in a book called *Roma 1943* by Paolo Monelli—a really wonderful, *vivid* book; a surprise, a marvel, in which he uses the line to show that in 1943 as in the time of the Belli, Romans had a hard time getting through life without swindling each other.

I had forgotten a third, less beautiful line, but what it says is much more Italian. It's one the partisan-tenor Ernani sings (as a prelude to the cabaletta "Aragonese vergine"). Particularly if the tenor has a good voice and sings it well, it represents the unfurling of our national flag to the sun: "Hear ye all the troubles of my heart."[5]

114

HEAR YE ALL THE TROUBLES OF MY HEART. Someday I will write and publish a very short story with that title. But not here and not now. Today

---

[3]"La bocca mi baciò tutto tremante." The words of Francesca da Rimini in Dante's *Inferno*. (V, 136)
[4]"L'uno buggera l'altro, Santità."
[5]"Udite tutti del mio cor gli affanni," from the opera *Ernani* by Verdi.

I have to write a different one. If I write two, the people on *Nuova Europa* will say I am abusing their hospitality.[6]

115

HE WHO—where? how? when? why? has lost contact with his own intuitive self; who is not able to see into himself clearly, by which I mean clearly into the very depths of his viscera, and even then, once returned to the surface, to laugh at what he has seen, and "pass beyond" it; he—like another friend of mine whom, this time, I refuse to name—can neither walk, nor jump, nor run. He can only flutter.

*

THIS, dear reader, is the very short story I promised you. You can (if you find you really need a title) call it "A Strange Customer."

I had, on that particular day, opened my store a little earlier than usual. Chiaretta, my assistant, hadn't come in yet. I was impatient for her arrival particularly because it was a cool, beautiful autumn morning and my friend Virgilio Giotti was to pick me up soon so that we could go out together.

The door opened. A man came in. He wanted to know the price of a book in the window, *Recollections of My Life* by Luigi Settembrini. I got the book (which, in fact, already had a price tag on it) and handed it to the man, saying, "It costs four lire, but for you, three and a half."

Then he turned around and looked at me. "But we know each other," he said.

We had in fact been introduced at the editorial office of *Popolo d'Italia* during the period of Italian neutrality before the First World War, which had ended fairly recently. I had only been back in Trieste for a short time. Then, while I wrapped the book for him, he asked me what I thought of the situation (this was toward the end of 1919 or 1920—I don't have much of a memory for dates). I gave him my opinion, and added—I wasn't, as you can see, a prophet—that Italy's guiding star would save us all from his ideas.

---

[6]The story appears on p. 211.

"And Dalmatia?" he asked me.

I answered that to wage a war to take Dalmatia would be like making love *deliberately* to get syphilis. Before I even finished the sentence, I remembered that he had, or had had, that illness (they said at the paper that he had contracted it as a young immigrant). But he didn't react, or didn't appear to. He picked up the book, his change, said good-bye, and left.

Chiaretta came in at that moment. She recognized him immediately from his photos in newspapers and magazines. Breathless from having run (Chiaretta was a diligent employee), she said, "Those violent types are very appealing to women."

Which perhaps meant that though she, Chiaretta, was by spirit and family history antifascist, she'd been instantly smitten by, or at least was interested in, that unusual early morning customer.

Rome
April–May 1945

Very Short Stories

1946

To the Reader

VERY SHORT STORIES are derived from shortcuts. They are really just shortcuts, a bit lengthened. This is how they came about.

I was reading the third series of shortcuts to my friend Giacomo Debenedetti. He listened through to the end, then said, "They're nice, but I'm not sure whether you realize something about them. Several have a different kind of rhythm. They're more like very short stories."

Even a critic—particularly if he does it casually and familiarly—can serve a purpose. My friend's legitimate observation was the Cesarean cut that separated one from the other.

I Saw Him

I SAW HIM FOR THE FIRST TIME when I was his age. He was seated, or rather crouched, near the railroad tracks. There were many people with him, all of them surrounded by parcels and packages. They were immigrants, an impoverished crowd watching with hate in their eyes as first-class trains passed them without slowing down, as though they didn't exist. But he was smiling.

I saw him several years later. He was legally my equal by then. During drills and long marches he would walk at my side and, from time to time, would smile at me. He didn't really know who I was, nor did I know who he was. I was just surprised that nothing seemed to surprise him.

I saw him during the war. He was frequently on troop trains, in encampments, and in trenches. He defended the Piave alongside comrades, more than one of whom could have been his father. He won the battle of Montello with boys of his own age. And he crossed and recrossed the Isonzo. When the armistice was signed, he wasn't surprised that the war was over (just as he hadn't been surprised when it broke out), nor that Italy had won it, and that it had, also with his valor, they told him, won Trieste and Trento. He recalled only that many of his companions had fallen, who, he said, would never return. They gave him, to keep him quiet (but he would have stayed quiet no matter what, even, I mean, if they hadn't given him anything), a small sum of money, and a huge kerchief printed with Italy's provinces and its new borders in the country's colors. He looked at it a long time, smiled, refolded it carefully, and put it away with his other things. After that I didn't see him for a number of years. Or at least I didn't want to recognize him.

I saw him again one recent evening in a depressing Roman tavern. He was sitting, the only youth (so young that to me, an old man by this time, he looked like a child) at a table with adults, who were recalling and carrying on about their old trenchmates. He was sipping slowly at a little red wine, and when they let him, he played cards. His chest was thinner, his shoulder blades somewhat sharp and projecting. He was wearing a faded military cap (you couldn't make out clearly which branch of service) at a sporty angle. His clothes were decent enough (it seems to me I heard he was working for the Americans). And his big boots were still enviable. No one paid any attention to him, least of all his companions, who only just answered him, and then not always. He smiled, didn't seem offended, and didn't react. With a barely noticeable movement of his hand, he would throw his cards, good or bad, onto the table. He seemed entranced, absorbed by an idea he surely didn't have: that he was just a poor, ordinary boy and the symbol of the mysterious joy of living. And perhaps of the Italian people.

Busy Little Kids

OUR "BUSY LITTLE KIDS," as newspapers call them with ironic indulgence, should feel like a plague of flies to American soldiers. However, it seems that's not always the case.

Today I saw one of them being arrested. A young American soldier was holding him, crying, by the sleeve. They had stopped in front of the main entrance of a requisitioned hotel. Soldiers and officers were continually walking in and out of the building without paying any attention to them. I don't know what the boy (he was about ten or eleven years old) had done or tried to do. I figured at least some petty theft. The soldier was speaking English, but no one in the crowd gathering around them could understand him, least of all his prisoner. The latter told anyone who bent over to ask him what had happened that he had done nothing, absolutely nothing, that he had been sitting there, right there (he pointed to the Triton fountain) when this guy here (the soldier) had suddenly jumped him and, without any reason, grabbed him. He was handsome, tattered, delicate, and agitated. But he wasn't really afraid. He'd been afraid for just one moment, when the American threatened that if he didn't keep quiet he would turn him over to the city police, who happened to be passing at the moment. Having understood the gestures, he'd kept quiet until he saw the police leave, then immediately began crying again. The soldier seemed very disconcerted by his prisoner—it was clear he didn't want to hurt him, yet letting the boy get away without some slight punishment would make it look as if he had given in to him, or perhaps complete impunity was repellent to his puritan soul. Meanwhile, other small boys (the square was alive with them) were organizing for a military rescue mission. They figured that if the soldier relaxed his grip, and if they were able to distract him for a moment, they could grab their friend and help him escape. There was even a plan of action. One of the boys, the oldest—he probably ran their "business activities"—made an aggressive move toward the soldier, hoping that the latter, in defending himself, would forget the other boy and in the ensuing confusion they'd both escape. But the American fought off the newcomer without letting go of his prey. So the operation ended in a general retreat with the group lurking at a safer distance from the hotel. Finally, after a quarter of an hour of lamentations and threats in various languages, the soldier decided to take the boy away. Where could he be taking him? He took him a few steps away to the military exchange. And what could he be doing with him? his friends, the public, and I wondered. After a minute, the boy came out alone. He was touching the back of his neck and sucking on something (gum? candy?). Every trace of unhappiness was gone from his face. He headed for his friends—a tiny sparrow toward other little sparrows, to resume his errant, temporarily lucky, life.

"The same at Tor di Nona," said Vigolo, to whom I told the story as he walked down the street with me. "Also at . . ."—and he named other places where there were black markets—"for people who know how to look for them, there are plenty of stories like that, full of warmth and compassion." But I wasn't thinking of Tor di Nona at that moment. I was thinking of the SS, of the Wehrmacht, and of the thousands of cohorts of that little boy whom the German soldiers everywhere in Europe, under the pretext of "blood laws" and other equally political and scientific "laws," had murdered. Or who had simply disappeared.

Madrigal for an English General

DURING THE EARLY DAYS OF THE ALLIED OCCUPATION I encountered an English general in Florence. He was, most uncommonly, on foot and drunk. And he was a wonder. Tall, thin, spare, shaved almost to the skin, he made his way, wavering unsteadily against the handle of a small, expensive-looking walking stick. Each person he passed could have, unintentionally, become his nemesis, caused him—a serious thing for anyone, a mortal blow for an Englishman of his rank—to lose his balance. But even under those circumstances, what bearing! What style! Like the British Empire, he could barely stay on his feet, but stay he did.

In Bologna

WHEN I WAS IN BOLOGNA IN 1913 I used to frequent a small café called At the Happy Europe. After a while I wondered how it got its strange name. The proprietor, who had taken over the place from someone else a long while before, didn't know. Eventually, a dear friend of mine, Giuseppe Paratico, a gentleman from Bologna, told me. The café had been opened immediately after the Napoleonic wars, when it was thought that the formation of the Holy Alliance had insured the end of warfare and would make poor Europe happy forever.

After the next war I returned to Bologna. The café was still there and so was my friend, though recently discharged from the service and impoverished. In 1928 I went back again. The little café, more squalid, more decrepit, and deserted because of competition from the many nearby bars (only two of its billiards players were alive), was still standing. But the friend who had revealed the mystery of its name was gone. "Killed," his beautiful widow told me, "by the horrors of fascism."

Reading of the liberation of Bologna (it finally happened!), of the flowers, the tears, the blood, the young girls clinging like grapes to heroes' trucks, I thought of the little café (perhaps under another name—the old one could have sounded subversive—it was still there and had had its day of celebration) and of that good, dear, courtly, crazy Paratico.

In Trieste

IN TRIESTE WHERE, WHEN I CAN'T SLEEP, I spend my nights worrying (God alone knows what this means!), I knew a young Yugoslavian woman about fifteen or twenty years ago.

Marizia was a good friend of my family's. She'd come by to see my daughter several times a day. They were both very young then and, as young girls often do, thought the world of each other and went everywhere together. For some reason though, Marizia was afraid of me. Nevertheless, one day she worked up the courage to accost me and ask if I'd read a book called *The Servant Bortolo and His Master,* which had just been translated into Italian. (I don't remember the name of the author—but there are so many other things I've forgotten these last, dreadful years!—I remember only that he was a Slovenian, born, I think, in Lubiana.) She told me that if I promised to read it, she would lend it to me. Then she asked me to read it carefully, because it was *the greatest book ever written in the whole world.*

She brought it to me the following day. The book (a small one, if I'm correct, from the Slavia collection) told the story of a Slovenian peasant, who, hoping for reparations for the wrongs done him by the young heir of his kind old master, boarded a railroad train bound for Vienna, where— like a child trusting in its father—he planned to present his case to Emperor Franz Joseph. But once in the large capital city, he never got to see the king, much less speak to him. Everyone to whom he turned for help either laughed in his face or sent him on a wild goose chase. When his money was gone (his entire life savings), he returned to his native region, where he died of a broken heart.

Though it may not be completely correct, that's my present recollection of the book. When I gave it back to the young girl, I thanked her for having acquainted me with the lovely little story which I told her I had indeed enjoyed, and whose author, I don't know why, had reminded me of our own Tozzi. I also told her (continuing down a wrong road) that there had been other writers in the world whose books were as good or even better, for example, to stay with novels, *The Betrothed* and, perhaps even better than that, *Crime and Punishment.* The girl stared at me with two large astonished eyes that suddenly clouded over, then averted mine at the same time that she broke into a wild laugh and fell frenzied and in a half faint onto a nearby couch. She was completely hysterical. My daughter began giving me hateful looks, and disapproval for what I had done was clearly written all over my wife's face. They had to get the girl water, revive her, and assure her that—as everyone knew—I was crazy, etc. etc.

So monstrous had an impartial judgment seemed to youthful nationalism.

Black Man

IN THE DAYS WHEN WE WERE CHEWING UP PEOPLE and one of those we were obliged to cut into little pieces and devour was the Negus,[1] I happened on a particular occasion to pass in front of a school hung with banners and closed for the day. The students, properly lined up under the guidance of their teachers, were out in the streets of Trieste that brilliant morning demonstrating their irrepressible patriotic and military fervor with shouts of "Death to the Negus," "Death to the Lion of Judah." It was to avoid hearing these jovial shouts (whose most distant consequences I foresaw), and to pass as few Blackshirts as possible on the way from my house to my store, that I had taken the lovely wooded and, I had hoped, deserted road on which that school stood.

But several of these lively youngsters had been left out of the procession—I don't know how or why—and were carrying on on their own near the school. They weren't even wearing the required Youth Corps uniform, and in the course of the episode I'm about to describe, two or three of them disappeared. The protagonist was a dark boy who was entertaining himself by drawing rapid charcoal caricatures of the Negus on the sidewalk. He would distort a few major aspects of the hated resemblance; add some nasty scrawls; then, followed by his pals, who called out remarks with somewhat embarrassed smiles, he would move a few steps away, find another good spot, and do the same drawing over again. Passersby looked down at his accomplishment with scant interest, then, to tell the truth, without uttering a word of criticism or comment, went on their way. Four or five times the student bent down to demonstrate his talent as a caricaturist. But—and this is what was curious—each time he finished his scrawling, he would get up and look around warily, as if he were afraid of something or someone. What made his behavior even stranger was that he would walk, looking backward, with his hands joined and crossed at the base of his back as if at any moment he expected to get a kick in the pants.

But why did this poor boy hate the Negus so much? And why, if he hated him so much, was he so afraid of him?

---

[1] Emperor of Ethiopia.

An idea, or perhaps it was a memory, helped me resolve this little problem. The Negus (in reality a great Oriental nobleman defending his homeland, whether acquired by inheritance or conquest, with exemplary dignity in the face of misfortune; and against whom it was possible to wage war without personal offense) was just the image to give new life, on an unconscious level, to a terrifying childhood image—that of a black man.

The analysis of our frightened caricaturist and of so many others, older and perhaps even more frightened than he, needs to begin at this point. But I'm breaking off here. If I didn't, this would no longer be a very short story.

The Turk

THE EPISODE I JUST RECOUNTED calls another to mind, though it has only a superficial relationship to the first. This one dates back to a much earlier time, and it didn't take place in the Viale XX Settembre in Trieste, but in the Piazza Vittorio Emanuele in Florence. Moreover, and I say this for my reader's peace of mind, it doesn't have an analytic point.

The war against Turkey had been declared that day or the previous one. It was an equally beautiful and luminous day, and I was crossing the square, I seem to recall, in the company of Aldo Palazzeschi.[1] Suddenly, the nineteenth-century air of which men and things still partook in those days was shattered by furious shouts of "Down with the Turk," "Get the Turk," "Death to the Turk."

A Turk in Florence?

Yes. He was one of those sidewalk vendors who hang around outside cafés and taverns, bothering people with their offers of carpets, pipes, and sundry odds and ends, and who (it may be said parenthetically) I had never seen conclude the smallest sale.

From all over, from the square and its adjacent streets, swarms of boys with nothing better to do were rushing at the enemy of the day (whom they had regarded the previous day with total indifference), and who now was attempting, as far as the merchandise he had in his arms and on his back permitted, to flee. Several passersby protested the attack (protesting malice wasn't yet a crime), but their words were completely useless. When the poor man found himself surrounded and without any means of escape, more to save his goods than his person (which wasn't in serious danger) he turned to his persecutors and spoke—who would have expected it?—in purest Tuscan. He was, as it turned out, a Florentine from San Frediano. He dressed as a Turk in the hope that his merchandise, like the Three Magi, would appear to have come from the Orient—though it really came, as did so many other falsities, from "friendly" Germany. He had also, the better to fool his customers, trained himself to speak and pronounce Italian incorrectly.

But as is always the case, there was a grain of truth on his pursuers'

---

[1] A poet and friend of Saba's, whose real name was Aldo Giurlani.

side. He himself told me, while catching his breath (he wasn't that young anymore) on a chair set out for him by Cesare (the famous waiter at the Giubbe Rosse), that he was indeed a native of San Frediano and that even his parents were born there, but one of his grandfathers (or great-grand-fathers, I'm not sure which) had moved from Florence to Smyrna. That's where he got the idea of dressing as a Turk and dealing in oriental goods. Why he hadn't doffed those dangerous clothes the last few days or why he hadn't stayed at home, I don't know and didn't ask. Perhaps he didn't even think of it. Perhaps he had relied—erroneously as it turned out—on his own good conscience.

You have just heard, as the radio announcer would say, an inauguration of the racial campaign.

Carletto and Military Service

BY NOW WE ALL KNOW THAT WAR IS A HORROR and not at all glorious. (If we had to build a monument to the recently ended war, it would have to be dedicated to women, not men.) Nevertheless, the fact remains that men do not hate war as much as they ought to. At least they don't hate military service, though they often complain about it. Most peoples (though surely Italians less than others) enjoy marching in ranks and singing "farewell, my beloved, farewell," and other such activities.

When my employee, "a lover of peaceful endeavors" as he once described himself to me, went for his first call-up (seventeen or eighteen years ago), he was, as the result of some previous illness, turned down. He returned from the encounter (for which he had armed himself with medical certificates and testimonial letters) dressed, as is proper for someone appearing before the authorities, in his best clothes. He told me immediately that he had been rejected, permanently rejected, and seemed pleased about it. Then he apologized for the few times he had angered me. He promised that from now on, he wouldn't do it again (at least, he added, intentionally); that hereafter, instead of wasting time and money at billiards, he would spend evenings at home studying French; that if I were as satisfied with him as he was with me, he would try to please me, and keep improving his knowledge of antiquarian books (all the more because, against all his expectations, he really liked the field); there were other sentimental pledges.

His exuberance spent, he returned to his work. That day it consisted of packing and crating books that had to be sent out of the country to a certain Mr. Polivka in Czechoslovakia. Time passed, perhaps half an hour. There was no other sound in our customerless store on the Via San Nicolò but the noise of a hammer nailing covers down on crates, while I typed the long letter that would accompany them. Suddenly, Carletto's voice interrupted me. "Signor Saba, if they had accepted me, in what branch would they have put me? I think the artillery." Another shorter silence, then, "Tell me, signor Saba, you were in the service. Is it true that it's so hard? Or is it true what I've heard, that in spite of the discipline, you can have a good time?" Silence again, followed by, "Who knows, if they'd taken me, to what wonderful place they might have sent me? Imagine, Signor Saba, a boy in my class who went in a year earlier than he had to, was sent to Rome." Brief silence for another little while, then, "They say that memories of military life stay with you forever, and are the best memories of your youth."

"Carletto," I said to him, "if you go on like this another minute, not only will you keep me from finishing this letter, you'll make me nostalgic for Petrarch."

"You," he answered, "whenever you say anything, it's always an insult."

But then, at closing time, as he was lowering the store's shutters, he let out that the preceding evening a female cousin had told him, "Men who aren't fit for the king, aren't fit for girls either."

And though wrongfully—his children prove the point today—at that moment Carletto was very humiliated and very hurt.

Celsa

CELSA IS EIGHTEEN YEARS OLD, the daughter of a tavernkeeper. She serves impatient men—civilians and soldiers—bread, wine, and food. Two of the tavern's windows were broken by Germans, one by a British soldier, one by an American. What's left of the place is worked over by neighborhood kids, who, from time to time, invade it, throw chairs around, then rush out shouting wildly. Celsa, like Mother Earth, endures all her children's wrongdoings. And, when she talks about them, smiles.

"Hear Ye All the Troubles of My Heart"

THOSE OF YOU WHO HAVE THE ADMIRABLE HABIT OF READING *Nuova Europa* may perhaps recall a shortcut of mine, in which I promised someday to write a brief tale about this most Italian line of poetry sung by the partisan-tenor Ernani the moment he steps on stage, and which, in my view, stands for our flag flying in the sun.

The trifling occurrence that will serve to illustrate this point took place when trains ran with a regularity that some already viewed with foreboding for Italy, and when the trip from Trieste to Milan took about six or seven hours.

A young girl entered a crowded third-class carriage, and immediately a young man got up and, in a rare act of courtesy for our times, offered her his seat. The girl refused, let herself be asked a few times, and finally, embarrassed but pleased, accepted. There was a short silence, some smiling back and forth, then the young man—as if it were his right as recompense for his courteous deed—began a conversation. He cut through the indispensable preliminaries and as quickly as possible got to the only thing that really concerned him: talking about himself. At first he spoke only to the girl, then slowly, as he became carried away with what he was saying, he told all the other passengers that he came from Milan, where he had his own small business which required frequent travel.

One evening while in Verona he went out to get something to eat in a trattoria. Seated at a nearby table was a girl who seemed unable to touch any of the food before her. She sighed, wept, and to the young man's surprise, cast pleading looks at him. He asked her if she was ill. She said no, but . . . but . . . she didn't have money to pay for her dinner. Her fiancé had walked out on her though they hadn't had even the smallest quarrel and now she was alone and without a cent in this city where she knew no one.

"These things happen," said the boy. And without bothering the waiter, he carried his food to the girl's table, sat down next to her, comforted her, and to get her to eat (but there was no need for that, he said, she ate as if she hadn't put anything in her mouth for two days) told her jokes and other "funny things." He paid the bill (he gave the amount, but repeating it these days it would read like fiction), and after that he took her to his hotel.

Now he had been living with her for two years. She was a very nice girl. She kept his things in order. She was grateful to him and concerned about him. She was also, and this was something he could swear to, faithful to him.

The problem that was tormenting him, and for which he seemed to be asking the public's advice, was should he or should he not marry her? His parents, who at first were furious with him, were now in favor of the marriage. He, however, was still hesitating. He was hesitating because he wanted the girl to give him a son before they married. Everyone was listening, laughing, discussing, and urging him to marry. Seeing the general interest that his story had created and that everybody except for a soldier sitting pensively in a corner seemed to think well of him, the boy took his wallet out of an inside jacket pocket, and out of the wallet, a photograph of a girl (rather pretty and clearly black), which he showed with a polite "May I?" to the girl to whom half an hour earlier he had given his seat. She, in turn, after having studied it at some length, asked his permission (which he readily gave) to show it to the other passengers. Several of them were already craning their necks. The photo, thus viewed, studied, discussed, passed from hand to hand, and—so to speak—pawed by all, was finally returned with several compliments to its owner, who now, having obtained what he had desired—the exposition of the troubles and joys of his simple heart to one and all—was smiling happily.

This is my very short story. Perhaps in a time of escape literature, and the yellow-jacketed editions of Treves, it could be called a "true life sketch." But—story or sketch—it is this incident, reclaimed for the first time from memory, which gives full meaning to Ernani's words.

An Old Man with a Beard

AN OLD MAN WITH A BEARD used to be a regular at the tavern in Rome where I take all my meals. Whether attracted to me by the similarity of our ages, or by a natural sociability, he was unprotected by any glimmer of sensitivity—something we've seen these last few years that has happened to others as well—and would persistently sit at my table and try talking to me. As I didn't reply, or answered only in monosyllables, he'd decide he'd made a bad choice. Right away his speech would become more formal. Right away he'd make some timid parting gestures.

Fortunately, one evening he asked if he could light his cigarette from my pipe, a favor I deny no one. "None so deaf," says the proverb, "as those who will not hear." I never saw him after that, not at my table, nor in the tavern, nor in the neighborhood. Perhaps he was hit by a car. Perhaps he'll never be in traffic again.

My Italy

WHEN YOUNG MICHELE HAS NO MONEY (his entire family, he says, was killed in the bombing of Cassino, but who knows if it's true), he still sits down at a table in the place I eat at regularly in Rome. But now he doesn't say anything or summon anyone. Instead, his eyes follow Celsa (all-powerful daughter of the owner and goddess of the place)—he hopes his gaze appears roguish, when it is really somewhere between ashamed and beseeching. Celsa, who has understood the situation perfectly, walks over to him (pretending not to have understood) and asks, "What do you want? Why are you looking at me that way?"

"I'm looking at you," is the boy's answer, "because you're so gorgeous."

Somewhat haughtily, and hiding her smile, Celsa serves him a half pint of wine, two small rolls, and whatever dish he chooses from the few—always the same—that the place offers daily. Michele eats hungrily and, when he has finished, turns to Celsa again. He wants her to give him his bill. He won't come back until he can pay what he owes, which he usually does in a day, two at the most. Once only (this winter) he stayed away for a month.

"What a pity," Celsa said to me then. "He's such a strange boy, but he seemed nice. Still, I never found out what he does or how he lives. And he's always alone. Did you see how he's dressed? Oh, that war!"

When, however, Michele has ready money, he becomes more demanding, or at least more impatient. In addition to his half pint of wine, he likes to have soda or an orange drink. But more than anything else, he wants instant service. He calls Celsa in a different tone of voice, pays her fewer compliments, and if she is delayed, he gets up, walks over to the small opening that faces the kitchen, parts the floral curtains, bends over, sticks his head through the opening, and leaning his elbows on the shelf, pesters Celsa's mother, who is the cook.

"Just take a look," Celsa said to me one day when, bringing my dinner, she'd come upon him doing just that. "Isn't he like a baby asking for the breast?" Michele turned at that moment, understood that we were speaking about him, and stuck his tongue halfway out.

"Such a big boy," Celsa went on in a loud voice, "almost ready to become a fighter" (she meant a soldier) "and he can't sit still for a minute."

Now That the War Is Over

THEY CAME IN BOLDLY AND LOUDLY, greeting people right and left, pretending they were certain (though they weren't) of being served like everyone else.

An announcement detested by all Allied troops was stuck onto the glass pane of a door. It was a ban. A circle (the horizon?); within the circle two crossed lines meant that the very establishment (trattoria, tavern, or bar) required to display it was obliterated from the face of the earth. How many dry throats, how many young hearts throughout the world have in recent years cursed that symbol? At first it was accompanied by the legend OUT OF BOUNDS, but that was subsequently thought to be superfluous, and dropped. In Celsa's tavern, though the poster had been placed fairly high up as a precaution, time and busy young hands had torn off a good two-thirds of it. But to convince themselves completely that "now that the war was over" there was no reason for the hateful prohibition to exist, certainly not in this visible form, one of the two Allied soldiers who entered tore off the other third. The extravagant act was his and his comrade's undoing.

Celsa's father, a big man, is committed to the rule of established authority (national or foreign), which, generally speaking, he obeys without question. But I think that, considering the circumstances and the decent appearance of the two young Americans, he would have for once (it would have been in his interest too) closed an eye. And I think that with his other eye, he would have shown them to a small adjoining room in which they would not only have been quietly on their own, but safe from the (not too attentive, to tell the truth) view of their military police. But that act had frightened him. He came out from behind the counter, where he was pouring allotted rations of wine for women and children who had proper cards for it, and confronted the two foreigners. He made them understand, more by gesture than by word, that what they had done was wrong, and that they had to leave his place immediately. But they already knew it. After trying uselessly to reattach the poster to the wall, they gave it, or what was left of it, back to him. Then they looked around seeking a bit of sympathy. They shook some hands, gave away some cigarettes. . . .

And humbly, abjectly, they went off toward their distant land.

Rome
March–June 1945

From Articles

Advice to Bibliophiles

THE PASSION FOR COLLECTING OBJECTS is as old as mankind. It satisfies a number of human proclivities, and once in a while suffices to fill an entire life.

But collecting antiquarian, or at least rare, books for those who have no specific goals can be very expensive and unending. This is why we advise bibliophiles to focus their interests and purchases with specific criteria in mind, that is, to decide to collect a certain category of book, and thereafter to deviate as little as possible from that choice. It goes without saying that the category may, indeed should, reflect the inclinations of the collector.

A near-complete library, that is, one which aims to acquire every important book published since the Gutenberg Bible, is the dream of an earlier age. Beyond the enormous expense based on the sky-high market value of books and other printed matter, one would need a palace wing to house the collection, a librarian to catalogue it, and a servant to dust it. A princely dream, in short, and as we've observed, one that is no longer attainable. A modern American millionaire, for example, with the strongest will in the world could not afford to collect the "plaquettes" of popular literature that one of the Parisian Rothschilds managed to put together in the nineteenth-century at a relatively modest cost. The crude engravings with which almost all of them were embellished didn't yet appeal to collectors, and hardly anyone was looking for them then.

By limiting a personal collection to only one category of book, the required space and expense are considerably reduced and the collector's pleasure becomes more focused and intense. Leaving out textbooks, of course, and popular literature (so-called cultural books, which are an ongoing necessity for the educated, but which have nothing or almost nothing to do with the true essence of bibliophilia), if the book lover concentrates on a specific category, lo and behold, things become clearer and easier for him.

One can start a collection in any of a number of categories. Among the most common and closest to people's hearts is the one called locality, which would include all the books, prints, and pamphlets that relate to the city or region of one's birth. If the subject is a small town, the process of collecting is both more difficult and easier. Easier because there is less material to acquire, more difficult because small towns have not aroused the interest over the centuries that Rome, for example, or Paris has, and the books that speak of them, the prints that illustrate them, are also fewer and therefore in most cases more expensive.

Other "restricted" collections (cited randomly) are aeronautics, alchemy, astrology, calligraphy, bird watching, chess and other games, geography, gymnastics, and so on to an infinite number of subjects. Memoirs that refer to a historical age in which the collector is particularly interested are also an excellent choice. And so are first editions, or at least fine and rare editions of great authors. One of the most fascinating and scarcest categories is that of schoolbooks (including storybooks, usually illustrated) from the sixteenth century through the first half of the twentieth and beyond. (In recent years I've had the opportunity to see several with colored illustrations printed around 1860 in England and Germany that were utterly delightful.) It is difficult, however, to find clean copies of these books. Most books used by children (catechisms, grammars, arithmetic and penmanship books, and so on) that haven't been completely destroyed are usually found in dreadful condition, disfigured by ink stains, primitive drawings in their margins, and other such things. Now, and this is a generality, the value of a book rises or falls in proportion to its state of conservation, which also explains why a book may appear in diverse catalogues with large variations in price. My advice to bibliophiles is to buy one book in perfect condition rather than ten damaged ones. It's a better investment for them and eventually for their heirs.

A collector may be particularly, even exclusively, devoted to books of a specific publisher; among the most popular, for example, are those issued by the Aldines in the sixteenth (extremely rare) and seventeenth centuries. In that case the subject of the book is of little importance. Concern is focused on the volume's internal condition—margins in particular, and external state—its binding. It is always preferable that bindings be contemporary, although particularly in the case of Aldines, there may be many justifiably recherché editions bound in nineteenth-century England, almost always in a colored morocco, sometimes in calf, with the Aldine anchor stamped in gold on the boards. They are quite elegant in this state. However, they've become very rare, almost impossible to find. Not one has passed through my hands since the Second World War.

The advice one can give bibliophiles is infinite. The little we've said is no more than the smallest part of what, if space permitted, one could say on the subject. But we prefer to say something now about how to buy books and about the price one should pay for them. Books on bibliography, beginning with the famous Brunet, later imitated with numerous additions by Graesse, are useful only up to a certain point, not so much because of inflation (one can correct for that with simple arithmetic), but because of the fact that some categories of books have grown enormously in interest, and therefore in value, while others have declined. Even bibliophilia is ruled by fashion. The fickle goddess who changes styles for women every season does the same for rare and antiquarian books at least once a decade. First editions of great authors are among those books that have risen most sharply in price in recent years. But this seems reasonable and understandable—something apart from the caprice of style—that goes beyond the simple desire to own and to collect. To hold, let's say, so unassuming a book as the first edition of Giacomo Leopardi's *Canti* in one's hands says something even to those who aren't true bibliophiles, and adds to our understanding of the author and his times.

It goes without saying that the dream of every bibliophile is to outsmart other collectors, that is to say, to find a valuable book at a bookstore or elsewhere being offered at next to nothing. The bibliophile's satisfaction is even greater (and unmixed with remorse) when, besting a book dealer (a not infrequent occurrence), he finds an item in a catalogue at a tiny fraction of its value and succeeds in obtaining it from the dealer, who is being bombarded with telegrams, phone calls, and express letters from other customers. I had a dear friend who, aided by good luck and his own talent, succeeded in putting together a choice and integrated collection of books, almost all of which were acquired at incredibly low prices.

But these situations don't occur very often, and the people who enjoy them seem somehow to be predestined for them. Thus my friend, who betook himself to a city that was celebrating the centenary of his favorite author, had barely stepped off the train and stopped at a bookstall, when instantly he turned up a first edition of that author, annotated in his own hand and offered at the price of a modern novel, if not less. It's like winning a sweepstakes or, to be up-to-date, a football pool. Situations, as we've observed, that one can't count on.

It is better to rely on antiquarian book dealers, who are generally more honest than people think (hardly any of them have gotten rich), and in particular on those who, after long experience gained most often at their own expense, have earned good reputations among others in the antiquarian book world. To obtain preference from a book dealer over his other clients (the items offered are usually single copies), it's wise to wire immediately on receiving the catalogue and to use a little prudent psychology. Never ask for a discount from the listed price; pay bills promptly (immediately on receipt of the invoice); don't unilaterally round out the amount of an invoice; and don't fuss over the slight but inevitable defects a book might have. Otherwise the bookseller, who is a businessman and merely human, will be tempted to reply to your request—should the same day's mail bring requests from other, more easygoing clients—with the word "sold." (Naturally, I am not speaking of myself. As is known, for many years now, the only thing I do for the bookshop that bears my name is prepare its catalogues.)

For his own guidance, the collector will find it very helpful to mark the price he paid in every book, using an erasable pencil. This is written on the fly leaf along with the date of the acquisition and the provenance. Above all, never write your own name, especially in ink on a frontispiece, something that is done more often than you'd think.

And to end this brief article with a tale, I will tell you about the time, many years ago, when I was called to Venice to purchase a library of about a hundred books on maritime subjects (another excellent specialized topic, especially for collectors whose lives are involved with the sea). Upon opening the first book, I saw that its frontispiece had been torn out. I thought it an accident and went on to a second, then a third. All had the same major defect; that is, each lacked its frontispiece. Hiding my irritation, I asked the person selling the collection (which without that defect would have had an enormous value) the cause of the incomprehensible mutilation. The fool told me that on the previous evening he had, himself, torn the frontispiece out of every book he intended to sell. The reason was that an ancestor, from whom the library had descended to him, had written his full name in ink on the frontispiece, and he didn't want it known that a member of his family in need of money, or simply because the collection did not interest him, had sold it. Thus, he had torn out the frontispieces with his own hands. "Books," he added, "are valued for their contents, not for their frontispieces."

I was, at that time, a little enamored of the profession by which I earned my living and I think I left that house without saying a word, without even nodding to the ingenuous iconoclast.

POETRY FROM THE SHEEP MEADOW PRESS

Desire for White
Allen Afterman (1991)

Early Poems
Yehuda Amichai (1983)

Travels
Yehuda Amichai (1986)

**Poems of Jerusalem and
Love Poems**
Yehuda Amichai (1992)

Father Fisheye
Peter Balakian (1979)

Sad Days of Light
Peter Balakian (1983)

Reply from Wilderness Island
Peter Balakian (1988)

5 A.M. in Beijing
Willis Barnstone (1987)

Wheat Among Bones
Mary Baron (1979)

The Secrets of the Tribe
Chana Bloch (1980)

The Past Keeps Changing
Chana Bloch (1992)

Memories of Love
Bohdan Boychuk (1989)

Brothers, I Loved You All
Hayden Carruth (1978)

Orchard Lamps
Ivan Drach (1978)

A Full Heart
Edward Field (1977)

Stars in My Eyes
Edward Field (1978)

New and Selected Poems
Edward Field (1987)

Embodiment
Arthur Gregor (1982)

Secret Citizen
Arthur Gregor (1989)

Nightwords
Samuel Hazo (1987)

Leaving the Door Open
David Ignatow (1984)

The Flaw
Yaedi Ignatow (1983)

The Ice Lizard
Judith Johnson (1992)

The Roman Quarry
David Jones (1981)

Claims
Shirley Kaufman (1984)

Summers of Vietnam
Mary Kinzie (1990)

The Wellfleet Whale
Stanley Kunitz (1983)

The Moonlit Upper Deckerina
Naomi Lazard (1977)

The Savantasse of
Montparnasse
Allen Mandelbaum (1987)

Aerial View of Louisiana
Cleopatra Mathis (1979)

The Bottom Land
Cleopatra Mathis (1983)

The Center for Cold Weather
Cleopatra Mathis (1989)

To Hold in My Hand
Hilda Morley (1983)

A Quarter Turn
Debra Nystrom (1991)

Ovid in Sicily
Ovid-translated by
Allen Mandelbaum (1986)

The Keeper of Sheep
Fernando Pessoa (1986)

Collected Poems
F. T. Prince (1979)

Later On
F. T. Prince (1983)

Walks in Rome
F. T. Prince (1987)

Dress of Fire
Dahlia Ravikovitch (1978)

The Window
Dahlia Ravikovitch (1989)

Whispering to Fool the Wind
Alberto Ríos (1982)

Five Indiscretions
Alberto Ríos (1985)

The Lime Orchard Woman
Alberto Ríos (1988)

Taps for Space
Aaron Rosen (1980)

Traces
Aaron Rosen (1991)

The Nowhere Steps
Mark Rudman (1990)

Hemispheres
Grace Schulman (1984)

Volte
Rebecca Seiferle (1993)

Divided Light:
Father and Son Poems
Edited by Jason Shinder (1983)

The Common Wages
Bruce Smith (1983)

Trilce
César Vallejo (1992)

Women Men
Paul Verlaine (1979)

The Courage of the Rainbow
Bronislava Volkova (1993)

Poems of B.R. Whiting
B.R. Whiting (1992)

Flogging the Czar
Robert Winner (1983)

Breakers
Ellen Wittlinger (1979)

Landlady and Tenant
Helen Wolfert (1979)

Sometimes
John Yau (1979)

Flowers of Ice
Imants Ziedonis (1987)

OTHER TITLES

Kabbalah and Consciousness
Allen Afterman (1992)

Collected Prose
Paul Celan (1986)

Dean Cuisine
Jack Greenberg and
James Vorenberg (1990)

**The Notebooks of
David Ignatow**
David Ignatow (1984)

**A Celebration for
Stanley Kunitz**
(1986)

**Interviews and Encounters
with Stanley Kunitz**
(1993)

The Stove and Other Stories
Jakov Lind (1983)

Two Plays
Howard Moss (1980)

Arshile Gorky
Harold Rosenberg (1985)

Literature and the Visual Arts
Edited by Mark Rudman (1989)

The Tales of Arturo Vivante
Arturo Vivante (1990)

**Will the Morning Be Any
Kinder than the Night?**
Irving Wexler (1991)

**The Summers of James and
Annie Wright**
James and Annie Wright (1981)